THE AGILE LEADER'S SCRAPBOOK

D/2018/45/6 – ISBN 978 94 014 4714 0 – NUR 810

Cover and interior design: Gert Degrande | De Witlofcompagnie

© Herman Van den Broeck, Barney Jordaan & Lannoo Publishers nv, Tielt, 2018.

LannooCampus Publishers is a subsidiary of Lannoo Publishers,
the book and multimedia division of Lannoo Publishers nv.

LannooCampus Publishers
Erasme Ruelensvest 179 box 101
3001 Leuven
Belgium
www.lannoocampus.com

HerMan van Den BRoeCk
BARNEy JORDAAN

THe Agilé
Leader's
SCRAPBOOK

LANNOO
CAMPUS

We dedicate this book to all leaders who
create value to make this world a better place for all.

To our partners, Greet and Mieke,
thank you for your contribution to this dream.

'Master, what are condor pairs thinking when
their youngsters leave the nest?'
'Nothing, really nothing,' said the Master.
'They're not thinking at all.
They look upon their young hopefully
and marvel at how they dive and spread their wings.
And even though their own bodies instinctively
follow the twists and turns,
they let their young fly on their own.
This is the moment the parents have been longing for:
to watch their young soar on the wings of their strengths.'

DARE TO BECOME AGILE!

This book challenges you to rethink the underlying assumptions
of the organisational principles you might
hold dear at the moment.

It invites you to take a critical look at
the sustainability of the managerial logic of the past 100 years
in the light of the turbulence, complexity and uncertainty
businesses of today experience.

Agility is a vast terrain.
It impacts organisational strategy and structure,
as well as operations and people.
Our focus is on eight agility challenges that leaders are commonly
confronted with and that span the entire organisational spectrum.

We hope that some of our assertions
will make you feel sufficiently uncomfortable
to stimulate fresh thinking
towards a better mobilisation of your own talents and skills
as well as those of your co-workers.

Agility

the ability to cope with
and influence environmental
changes in a fast, innovative and
sustainable way

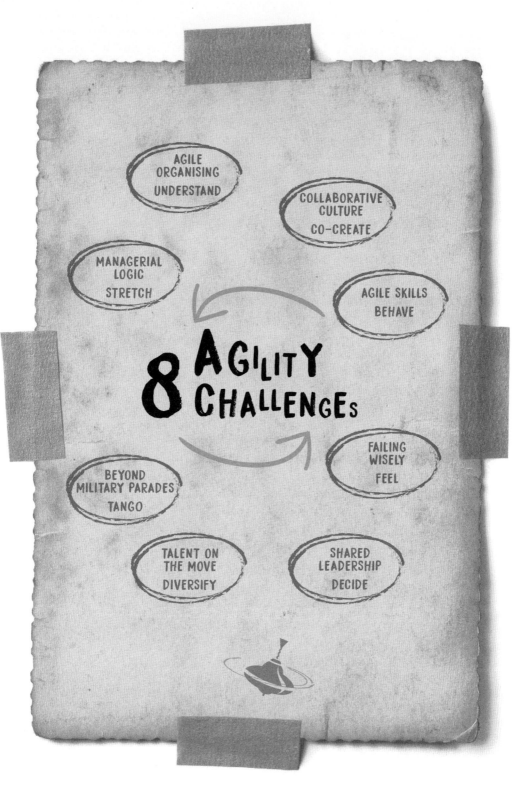

CONTENT

Stretching your managerial logic 11

11 | Agility: the talk of the town
13 | Shaking the foundations
14 | Perfection kills creativity
15 | Trees graced with wings?
16 | The great irony: agility needs stability (and vice versa)
18 | Rooting and soaring: a great 'living-apart-together' relationship
20 | Get clear on where your organisation sits right now
26 | Four different mindsets: take the test!
30 | Mastering agility

Understanding agile organising 35

36 | Four key characteristics: get fascinated by fractals
39 | The organisational cancer of the past: positional organising
41 | Managers of links, not of things
45 | Integrated data systems: a necessity
46 | Useful slack: deliberate inefficiency pays off
49 | A waste of money?
49 | Go on a blind DATE: DAre to Trust and Empower
51 | Rehabilitating the ugly duckling

In need of a collaborative culture 59

59 | Meetings are like traffic jams
62 | Get rid of that old-fashioned meeting style
63 | The future is co-creation
64 | Developing a collaborative space

Skills clusters for soaring 73

74 | Decision-making principles for soaring
75 | Three critical skillsets
78 | How to? Cluster 1: Authentic connection
83 | How to? Cluster 2: Divergent thinking
89 | How to? Cluster 3: Constructively dealing with differences
91 | Bye-bye SMART, hello CONDOR

The art of failing wisely 97

99 | Instil a growth mindset
100 | Seven key characteristics of a growth mindset
106 | Building resilience: learning to cope with mistakes
110 | Be aware of your decision-making biases

Towards shared leadership 117

118 | Conquering our Stone Age mindset
120 | A leader should create space and opportunities for soaring
122 | Your choice: sharing leadership, or running with
the power mongers?
123 | Implementing a shared leadership approach
126 | Co-create for real change
128 | Just remember

Talent on the move 133

133 | In need of a complete makeover
136 | Five tough questions to ask, five assumptions to let go of
143 | So, do we just ignore the human element?

From military parades to dancing the tango 149

150 | Don't collapse under the weight of complexity:
abandon the illusion that creating one big,
uniform organisation will save costs
151 | Conquer the Olympian peak: create a space for rooting
and soaring to coexist
152 | Don't be dependent on power mongering while innovating:
hire a sniper to get rid of your 'murder' boards
154 | Time to tango

158 | Notes and extra reading

165 | Quotes

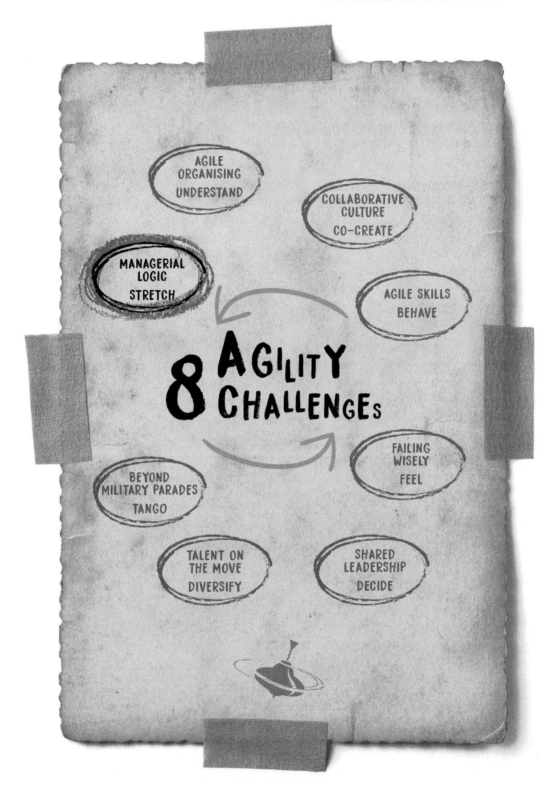

AGILITY CHALLENGE 1

Stretching YOUR MANAGERIAL logic

Agility: the talk of the town

Everyone is talking about agility, but what does it really mean? And why should you turn your highly structured organisation or department into a flexible and nimble unit? Because agility is the flavour of the month? Certainly not!

The concept of 'the agile organisation' is not new.[1] The importance of agility to organisations has been preached before. In the 1990s the principles of the 'learning organisation' were seen as a nice add-on to management practices, which clung to linear thinking patterns – as if all the complexity out there could be reduced to a simplistic five-step model! If you still believe this, we would, as a start, invite you to throw that idea overboard.[2]

You can't ignore the fact that globalisation and the acceleration of technological innovation have created a **VUCA** world which seriously challenges prevailing notions of management systems and leadership.[3]

VOLATILE
UNCERTAIN
COMPLEX
AMBIGUOUS

Speeding up while at the same time maintaining the highest quality standards has become the biggest challenge for organisations of all kinds.[4] The key question is: How can your organisation not only survive, but also grow and thrive in today's volatile reality?

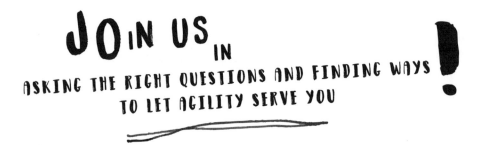

JOIN US IN ASKING THE RIGHT QUESTIONS AND FINDING WAYS TO LET AGILITY SERVE YOU!

Shaking the foundations

The aim of this book is to make you think about how to introduce agility into your organisation without throwing stability completely overboard. We acknowledge that just *thinking* about agility may frighten you. Creating an agile workplace will lead you to question your current operational processes; it may also challenge your need to keep control, bring up fears of losing power and play havoc with your well-being. You will feel unsure about the impact on, for example, your organisational culture, market position and budgetary implications. In short: introducing agility creates *uncertainty* about the future – your own but also that of your organisation. Rather than neglecting or complaining about this feeling, can you frame it as a great opportunity to become even more impactful? Can you redefine the steep change curve as a great opportunity curve? The frame you adopt will determine the choices you make and therefore the success or failure of your efforts.

If leaders can't overcome their fear of becoming agile, they will straitjacket their co-workers.

Their organisation will continue to walk well-trodden paths and miss the golden opportunities a VUCA world offers.

You need to realise that the tight rules and structures and accompanying control systems that in the past provided long term stability and security, now make your organisation fragile because it is unable to respond quickly to threats and opportunities present in the ecosystem you operate in. Every rule, every structure, every silo is a hurdle that makes change more difficult.

Perfection kills creativity

Most organisations are set up in a way that inhibits change.[5] We are genetically coded to 'protect' ourselves against threats and we do this by creating as much predictability as possible. No wonder then, that we prefer to organise for repeatable, 'safe' processes.

Indeed, looking at the Western managerial rhetoric of the past 100 years, the emphasis has been on creating profitability through standardisation, stability and predictability; on maximising profit through tight regulation of and control over work processes, over the means of production, and over employees. Creating those strong roots – 'rooting' the organisation – was management's ultimate objective. Even today, we are brainwashed into this traditional mindset.

This mindset has its drawbacks. Meaningful in a context characterised by a slow pace of innovation, it tries to ensure perfection by eliminating errors. But in so doing, it straitjackets people into standardisation, suppresses innovation and creates fear of failure – the very things that kill entrepreneurship. Concentrating only on the rooting process of your organisation makes you rigid and blind to alternative (and often better) ways of doing things.

NATURE IS PERFECTLY IMPERFECT

Nature requires living organisms to adapt to changes in the environment in order to survive. Those that fail to adapt, do not survive.

Bernd Heinrich, in his intriguing book *The Homing Instinct*, writes that Mother Nature understands quite well that perfect mechanisms, in the long term, do not provide the best results. And so Heinrich seconds Voltaire, the French philosopher, when the latter says, 'Le mieux est l'ennemi du bien' ('The best is the enemy of the good').

Salmon, with almost perfect accuracy, can smell and return to their spawning streams of origin. Close to perfection? Indeed. In one experiment, 90% of the salmon selected the stream with the 'smell of home'. What about those that did not make it to their home turf? These 'imperfect' ones often adapted to other environments, sometimes even finding *better* environments to breed in. For the long-term survival of the species, it is good not to be perfect! Imperfection, therefore, is nature's way of helping us to adjust to a changing environment.

IN TODAY'S MANAGERIAL LANDSCAPE, WE HAD BETTER REMEMBER THIS!

'**B**ecause our environment is changing faster than ever, trying to optimise for perfection is becoming a fool's game.'

S. Paju[6]

Trees graced with wings?

For a long time, rooting was a good strategy. A stable environment allowed you to rely on your analytical competences to plan for the future with a reasonable degree of certainty. Managing was not too difficult: you had time to plan, time to adjust, even the time to carry the costs of internal political games. Those times are gone.

In a VUCA world, the tighter you make the controls – driven by the illusion that everything can be predicted – the more fragile the organisation becomes. Leading organisations combine strong roots (standardisation and control) with adaptability, dynamism, speed and flexibility ('wings') so that they can also soar; that is, be agile.

Soaring allows you to explore, and adapt at speed if necessary. It is characterised by high levels of autonomy for people across the organisation, trusting co-workers to be entrepreneurial and get on with it. All of this is supported by 'loosely coupled' structures to ensure dynamic rather than tight control.[7] Agility 'is the new efficiency'.[8] Indeed, the need for organisations to become agile is here to stay. It means, though, that leaders and managers need both a new mindset and skillset.

Agile leaders create the space to soar. Are you up to the task?

A PENNY FOR MY OWN THOUGHTS

The great irony: agility needs stability (and vice versa)

Organising well is about finding the sweet spot between 'rooting' and 'soaring'.[9] The higher the level of volatility in your organisation's ecosystem, the less tightly structured ('coupled') you need to be to enable 'soaring'. The more stable your environment, the more rooted your organisation – or those parts that are predictable and stable – should be.

Should you try to make that which needs to be rooted more agile, you will end up without a proper structure (i.e. not grounded) and therefore unable to deliver the necessary standardised products and/or services. If, on the other hand, you try to root that which needs to be agile, you will become very fragile, unable to react to changes in the environment.

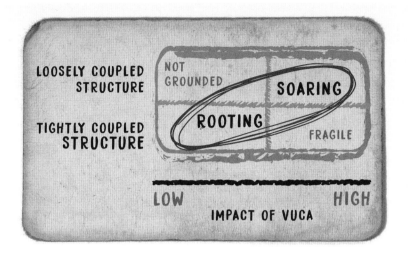

THE STORY OF THE TANDEM HITCH

At a horse and carriage parade in a resort town on Belgium's North Sea coast, we were fortunate to have an expert close at hand as we watched the graceful procession. We were particularly intrigued by a carriage being pulled by two horses one behind the other, and not alongside each other, as is usually the case. Our expert explained the thinking behind this 'tandem hitch'. The horse closest to the carriage, attached firmly to the carriage shafts, is the 'wheeler'. This is the stronger of the two horses and it does most of the work. The other horse, the 'lead horse', is only loosely coupled with leather straps, and runs relatively freely in front of the wheeler. In days gone by, the idea was that the lead horse should do little work on the journey to the venue for the day's hunt, so that it could arrive fresh before being uncoupled, saddled and used for the hunt proper. The wheeler, who had done all the hard pulling, was left behind, still firmly strapped to the carriage.

Applied to an organisation, the wheeler represents the fixed company structure, which is necessary for the predictable

| work based on acquired knowledge and routines. But this
| structure alone is insufficient to provide the enthusiasm,
| freshness and flexibility required to explore the new horizons
| of the 'hunting ground'. This requires a lead horse that roams
| free and relatively unrestricted.

Rooting and soaring: a great 'living-apart-together' relationship

The relationship between *rooting* and *soaring* can be seen as a great LAT (living-apart-together) relationship. It is not a symbiotic one, nor are the two elements necessarily in perfect proportion. Let us explain.

First, rooting and soaring, although seemingly contradictory, are not – and should not be – at odds with each other. Your organisation must be both stable and agile, not simply the one or the other. It must 'straddle' the two. The reality is that we frequently encounter organisations in which the wings and the roots compete with, rather than leverage and augment, each other.

Another common problem is that organisations try to tackle their challenge to become agile with the trusted old weapon of standardisation! This is nonsense. Once caught up in the turbulence of a VUCA world, an innovative and entrepreneurial organisation offers more, not less, freedom to co-workers and less, not more, structure and control. The 'agile logic' allows bottom-up, self-organised, goal-oriented activity to emerge.[10] Within this logic, you *win* by controlling co-creation processes; you *lose* when you control people.[11]

Thirdly, you have to ban umbrella concepts such as 'efficiency' and 'effectiveness' from your jargon: they describe everything, yet mean nothing. Why? Well, because these concepts in particular are the idols of rooting; they equate to standardised quality, driven by rules and regulations.

When you promote them in an undifferentiated manner, you are telling people that an organisation will only survive if it has firm roots; in doing so you are (implicitly) restricting them from soaring!

JUST TRY IT MAY CHANGE YOUR LIFE

BE MORE PLAYFUL

Whenever your boss uses the words 'efficient' or 'effective', you should shout 'bullshit!'.
Make clear that you don't understand what your boss really means: does he want more of the same (stronger roots) or a new and innovative approach (soaring to explore)?[12]

Fourthly, be careful of the kind of thinking that wants to perfectly 'balance' rooting and soaring or see it as another organisational formula. Depending on your context, you might need to root more at certain times, while soaring more at other times. Remember that a period of stability offers an excellent opportunity to prepare for soaring – and during a period of soaring, it is probably time to prepare for rooting!

Finally, remember that new information technologies – while they might provide smart integrated data – on their own aren't sufficient to make you agile! Such technologies will in the near future turn all kinds of organisations into 'smart' ones, but becoming smart is as important for soaring as it is for rooting. Smart organisations get rid of silo databases in favour of integrated ones, thereby also showing how decisions impact the broader ecosystem. They provide integrated, readily available and end-to-end data that can accelerate decision making. Within rooting, these smart feedback loops make a lot of change processes obsolete because continuous adjustments become real time. Within soaring, smart data provides the necessary integrated data to be able to go beyond the status quo.

Smart information systems are merely tools to sustain decision-making processes, they do not, of themselves, make the organisation agile.

Get clear on where your organisation sits right now

To better understand the underlying differences between establishing *stability* and supporting *agility*, you as a leader first need to be clear about your position on two key dimensions. The first, which will come as no surprise, is your position along the 'soaring'–'rooting' continuum. The second is about the kind of impact (added value) you want to have.

STRADDLING SOARING ⬅➡ ROOTING

How open to interpretation should you leave the implementation (the 'what and the how') of managerial decisions? Should you empower and trust your co-workers to be entrepreneurial and to explore new horizons, while relying on their strengths ('soaring')? Or should you tightly anchor operations, meticulously prescribing to co-workers what must be done ('rooting')?

To find the answer, ask yourself how stable and predictable your product, service, operating environment, client segment and applied technology are at the moment. If the information at your disposal tells you that these are all stable and predictable, you can best invest in operational excellence; that is, *build for consistency – continuity – stability – realism – certainty – standardisation – compliance*. So, you 'root'.

The moment you have any uncertainty or lack of clarity on this question, you should shift to the left of the spectrum: *design for entrepreneurship – exploration – innovation – disruption – trial-and-error – risk taking – nimbleness;* that is, allow co-workers to 'soar'. Guided by a clear vision and some agile decision-making principles, co-workers should be allowed to form small, multidisciplinary teams to collect and share information, as well as develop innovative and disruptive ideas and be given space and resources to experiment with these. Tap their hidden talents and allow them to take off and soar to new horizons.

Soaring is about dealing with, and even influencing, environmental changes in a fast, graceful and innovative way. It is characterised by an alertness to changes in the environment through frontal and peripheral vision, combined with the ability to rapidly adjust direction. It allows for progress despite uncertainty and helps to adapt 'on the go'.

SOARING ⟵⟶ ROOTING

How painful is this straddling for you?

Do you have endless discussions between rooters and soarers about alleged unfairness when some get a more flexible regime than others? Complaints from your innovative project teams that they are suffocated by the confines of the rooting logic? Don't you have any alternatives to move beyond your traditional rooting tools and concepts in your attempt to become more agile? Ideally, you shouldn't be having these kinds of discussions because it isn't about whether rooting or soaring is better – this is typical 'either-or' thinking. You should rather think 'and-and' as rooting and soaring can go hand-in-hand. Here's an example a frustrated HR officer shared with us where a rooting logic prevailed over an opportunity to introduce flexible work practices (i.e., soaring):

> 'Top management together with the unions decided to allow people to work from home from time to time. Yet we had to install a tight control procedure. Co-workers have to apply well in advance and in a prescribed form – approved by their boss – explaining precisely what they will do at home. If approved, strict terms are imposed (e.g. ½ day a week). Why can't we just trust our co-workers to decide among themselves? This will help each case to be judged on its own merits in a way that accommodates the individual's and the team's needs to ensure that the job gets done. But management and unions are very short-sighted when it comes to empowering our co-workers.'

STRADDLING: EXPANDING VALUE ⟷ PULLING IN VALUE

Whether you are soaring or rooting, your aim is to have impact and to create sustainable value, correct? We refer to this as your 'ripple effect'. Unfortunately, 'value creation' is yet another umbrella concept of the traditional managerial jargon. What does it mean? Value for whom? Is the goal to optimise value for the organisation and its shareholders so that it can be stronger, better and more profitable than all the rest – in other words 'pulling in value'? Or are you looking for sustainability by creating added value for a broader whole? In other words, a holistic eco-perspective whereby you are 'expanding value' both within and beyond the organisation?

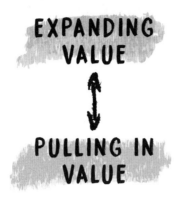

How painful is this straddling for you?

What's good for one element (individual or unit) is not necessarily good for the system (company or society). Conversely, what's good for the system is not necessarily good for the element. This is what an IT manager told us:

> 'My co-workers highly appreciate the fact that I managed to increase our budget for the coming year. But the consequence is that all other departments had to reduce own budgets. My co-workers know I'm not a solo player, I do my best for my team. Yet through the eyes of my peers, I'm quite selfish and short-term oriented. I find it difficult to collaborate to maximise value for all concerned.'

Sounds familiar? As you will discover later (see part 2), you need to be concerned about the 'ripple' effect of your decisions through the whole value chain, and not merely care about short-term goals like increasing this year's budget or maximising short-term profits for shareholders (who are often nameless and only have fleeting relationships with your organisation).[13]

BEATING OR BEAUTIFYING THE WORLD?

An ancient noble once sent his daughter to study the art of fighting. She was sent to the Master of Masters, the one who had mastered all fighting sports, the bravest of all. On arrival at the monastery, she asked the tallest man: 'Are you the Master of Masters?'

'No,' the man said, 'you'll find him over there.'

At the entrance to the garden, she found a very muscular man and asked: 'Are you the one?'

'Certainly not,' the muscular man replied and told her to enter the garden. A little man was doing some gardening, and she asked: 'Where can I find the Master of Masters?'

The gardener replied that he did not have the time to take her to the Master as he had to look after the roses. If she could help him out, he said, he would introduce her to the Master later.

A bit doubtful at first, she nonetheless started to prune the roses, commenting on the beauty of the garden. Just then, she got pricked by a thorn, and her finger started bleeding slightly.

'Be careful,' the gardener said, 'little details make the difference, and what's more, there are no roses without thorns.'

The noble's daughter continued pruning, now concentrating much better on her work. A half hour later the gardener asked her: 'What are you doing?'

'Pruning these roses.'

'Perhaps not,' he said, confusing her. 'Take a closer look from 10 steps away.'

'A closer look from further away?' she asked herself. 'How is that possible?' Seeing the big wall covered with roses, she understood she was beautifying the wall of the monastery.

'Now you are ready to learn,' the gardener said. 'The secret of mastering something lies in paying full attention to the detail, while never forgetting the big picture. Go now and start your fight.'

Walking away from the gardener she asked a passer-by: 'Where can I find the Master of Masters?'
'You just worked with him for half a day,' came the reply.
If you keep on learning while seeing the big picture and not forgetting the important details of today, you will also become a Master...

Author unknown[14]

Four different mindsets: take the test!

In the figure below, we bring both straddle approaches together, ending up with four different managerial logics. The two on the right-hand side of the figure suggest a need for rooting, while the two on the left reflect a need for soaring.

Our experience with coaching top teams has taught us that most teams are vague about the managerial logic they apply. Consequently, organisations are implicitly moulded by managers and leaders with different managerial logics. Although many logics do have their uses, our tendency is to assert the correctness of our logic and force it upon others, independent of the needs of the context. Managing people is not about imposing your managerial logic, but about strategically *choosing the logic needed for the moment*.

If we were to offer you one of the following jobs, which would you choose?

1. A role that requires you to search for innovative solutions that create a sustainable impact going beyond your project team, and perhaps even beyond your organisation.
2. A job that requires you to come up with a standardised sustainable solution that is repeatable in the long term.
3. A role challenging you to be disruptive and to give a creative answer to a unique opportunity, which could be the beginning of a great adventure.
4. A job that requires a sound solution based upon the key rules and practices of the organisation with a considerable profit and loss ratio strengthening your position?

Have you made your decision? Now read about the underlying logic of each alternative.

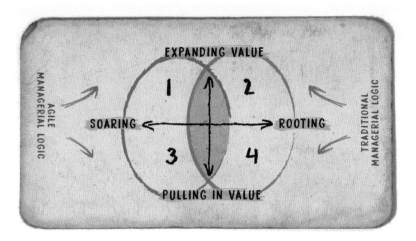

MINDSET 1

Cooperative – caring – project work: open experimentation within a sustainable vision. You want to spend time on what makes sense for you, your team, your organisation and society. You are passionate about contributing and strongly believe in reciprocity – if you give, you will get. You want to co-create for the better, are very open to feedback and can adapt easily when required. Co-workers shouldn't be treated as numbers, but as human beings keen to realise their talents.

YOUR MAXIM? An innovative contribution
towards a meaningful purpose.

MINDSET 2

Fair – sound – well-structured: a sound structure guarantees operational excellence and internal and external fairness. Co-workers should have equal opportunities based on objective criteria to build their careers. Each organisation has to fulfil its specific role (mission) in society. An ideal environment is one where you can do the right thing from the start. Because the system can be trusted, people can work at ease without having to watch their backs.

YOUR MAXIM? Organise things thoroughly,
and enjoy your position as an expert.

MINDSET 3

Playful – daring – unique: you like disruptive ideas, products and services. You welcome unique ideas that go beyond the known. You realise that with 10 great ideas, only one will be a real winner… so, let 1000 ideas bloom! Co-workers should surprise you and their peers with innovative and entrepreneurial ideas. Sometimes you win, sometimes you lose. You persevere, until you've reached your '*moment de gloire*'. Those who inspire you are welcomed. As a real entrepreneur, you 'fail forward'.

YOUR MAXIM? Hit the road, because not daring to act is more dangerous than trying out new things!

MINDSET 4

Competitive targets – no-nonsense: stick to what brings in the money and keep searching for even more profitability. The best performers get their rewards; those who cannot keep up, should look for another job. In highly demanding and competitive environments, be nice to everyone, but trust no one. You go for repeat business with a high profit margin, and work only with high achievers.

YOUR MAXIM? Eat or be eaten.

ASSIGNMENT: CHALLENGE YOURSELF AND YOUR TEAM!

In the quadrants above, draw the following symbols:

 where you feel most at home

 what you are paid/rewarded for

 where your company profiles itself towards its external clients

a. With your peers, discuss each other's preferred spots (where you feel most at home). How have these different positions caused tensions in the past? Try to understand each other's logic, and learn from it.
b. How appropriate are your current mindsets for the challenges your organisation currently faces?
c. Would you dare to do this exercise with your management team or board?

Explore and enjoy the tension caused by these two straddles and see them as opportunities to develop enhanced perspectives rather than adopting a 'one way only' mentality in favour of a particular managerial logic. Next time you are in a meeting, observe how the participants wrestle with these two essential choices when they try to solve problems, usually without articulating their underlying mindsets.

Mastering agility

Mastering agility does not neglect the importance of *rooting* – quite the opposite. Great organising is not about choosing the one over the other; most of the time you need both. The only thing you should *not* do is implement the one with the toolkit of the other!

Mastering agility is aimed at creating an organisation of internal cross-cutting networks that operate with little to no interference, yet are supported by a clear vision and appropriate decision-making rules and tools. Soaring is about leaders 'letting go': trusting people and providing them with a high degree of autonomy to take decisions quickly. It is also about expecting and allowing people to sometimes fail in their pursuit of innovation. What follows in this book will make this clear to you.

Challenge your thinking !

Question 1

✳ *Still obsessed with chasing perfection, while your efforts should be focused on skilful adaptation?*

✳ *Is it clear in terms of the above 4 managerial mindsets what the current dominant spot of your company and teams should be?*

Question 2

✳ *Smooth rooters often lack the skills for smooth soaring. Yet most boards of companies are populated with leaders who have built up their experience grounded in rooting. Is it time to bring in fresh blood?*

Question 3

✳ *Where do you apply the rooting logic, when you should be applying the soaring logic?*

✳ *Who are the people to help you improve the conditions for soaring in your company?*

Make your choice, stay where you are OR TAKE THE LEAP !

What the others make of
my actions is their business,
not my responsibility.
Anyway, our evaluation system asks me
only to account for what I do within my job.

OR

We all feel responsible for the impact
of our decisions on others.
Feedback is mainly about impact,
not intentions.
We've expelled the foolish linear logic
whereby those who save the most
get the highest reward.
Our reward systems, in the first place,
value the contributions
we make to others.

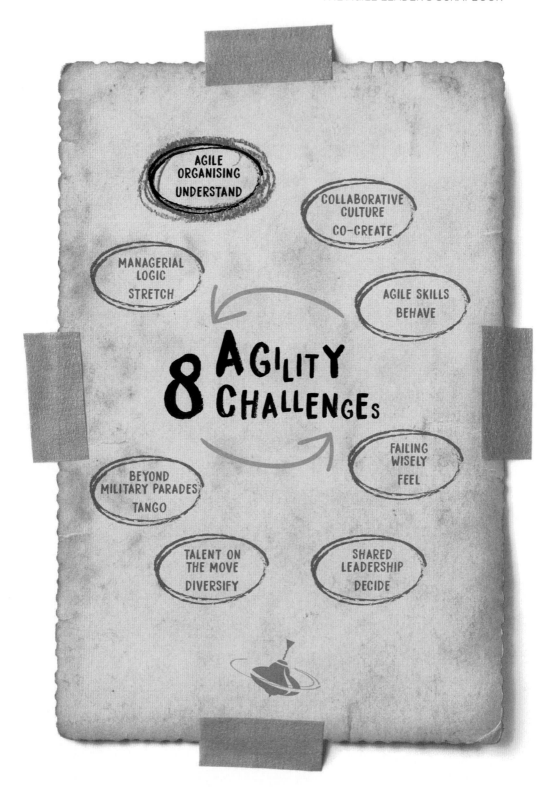

AGILITY
CHALLENGE **2**

Understanding
AGILE
organising

Open the curtains one winter morning and you may find yourself amazed by the beauty of a landscape blanketed by fresh snow. There has been no manager, no leader, no hierarchy and no imposed system that orchestrated this effect, yet the beauty and symmetry of the snowy scene is always picture perfect, isn't it?

Is this a case of quality created from nothing? No, absolutely not. So how do such self-steering systems work? Join us in trying to *unravel the characteristics of agile organising.*

Four key characteristics: get fascinated by fractals[15]

A human being grows out of only two cells which then multiply; a fern consists of a small pattern which is repeated multiple times – the same is true for broccoli and snowflakes. They all follow the same logic: repeated small patterns.[16]

To begin with, growing from within needs a **minimal, basic structure**. This entity is called 'a fractal'.[17] The multiplication of this fractal eventually forms the beauty of the broader well-functioning structure and that multiplication process is governed by only a few rules. In nature, there are many examples of such structures. Think, for example, of a flock of birds or a school of dolphins flying or swimming together without colliding.[18]

Similarly, agile organisations are composed of small autonomous teams guided by a limited number of **basic decision-making principles**. The more rules there are to be followed, the bigger the hurdles to navigate, the slower you become and the more difficult it is to adapt. Certain rules might be suitable for a rooting environment, because you expect the environment to remain stable and want standardised outputs. But the same toolkit will hamstring you if you need to soar to explore and innovate, and especially when you want to speed up.

Thirdly, agile organisations are also **'loosely coupled'**. When you want to soar, the links between teams and organisational units must be 'loosely coupled' and not locked in to a strictly imposed hierarchy. In this way, the entrepreneurial capacity of the teams is not restricted.[19] *Loosely coupled organisations* consist of teams and units that have enough freedom (loose) to be able to go their own way, while at the same time being connected enough (coupled) to serve the greater whole.

> 'Netflix has only two types of rules: those designed to prevent irrevocable disaster and those designed to prevent moral, ethical and legal issues. It has no vacation policy and does no tracking of time – the company's focus is on what needs to get done, not how many hours or days are worked.'[20]

Easy to say, but how do you make sure all this freedom doesn't erode all that is healthily stable? Well, you will only achieve this if co-workers identify with and feel passionate about the company's vision! So, the fourth characteristic is having and sharing **a passionate vision**. Although there may be variety in our daily weather patterns, there is an overarching logic guiding it, namely the rhythm of the seasons. In chaos theory, this kind of metalogic is called 'the strange attractor'.[21] For individuals, their personal values serve as the strange attractor of their behaviour (thinking and doing). In organisations, a 'passionate vision' does the same. It provides the beacons to stay aligned, allowing for a variety of formats and behaviours, while in pursuit of a common dream.

'If you want to build a ship,
don't drum up people together to
collect wood and don't assign them
tasks and work, but teach them to long
for the endless immensity of the sea.'
—Antoine de Saint-Exupèry[22]

When you need to soar, lack of a passionate vision will be fatal. A clear and heartfelt vision creates space and the beacons between which your co-workers can soar freely to discover new ideas and opportunities. If co-workers don't 'long for the sea', the slightest wind will send them off track. Their actions will be guided by their own individual strange attractor and your organisation will end up going everywhere and, consequently, nowhere. You will not be able to trust their decisions, nor their actions, and stricter and multiple controls will become a necessity. You will have to root them, thereby choking their innovative talent.

A shared vision allows you to empower people; it motivates them and stimulates entrepreneurship, creativity and engagement. It rubs off! And on top of that (paraphrasing Kenney): When an organisation has a shared vision, different internal stakeholders are less able to let their silo mentalities be a roadblock to the adaptiveness of the company as a whole in the face of rapid change.[23]

Does your organisation radiate such a vision? Not one that is mere window dressing, or looks nice on your website, but one that is authentic?

You might think that having a shared vision is not a necessity if you are rooting, because your organisation's tight control systems will make co-workers stay on course. They may *have* to stay in the rut of the path, but the question remains: do they *want* to do so? We don't need to remind you what it costs to have uninvolved and disengaged employees! A passionate vision provides for involvement and engagement. Without it, you will need all kinds of bells and whistles to get your co-workers to do what they have to.

ꜰꜰꜰꜰ ꜰꜰꜰꜰ ꜰꜰ ꜰꜰꜰꜰꜰꜰ ꜰꜰꜰꜰꜰꜰꜰꜰꜰꜰꜰꜰꜰꜰꜰꜰꜰꜰꜰ

HOW TO DEEPEN THE VISION OF YOUR TEAM

Start with a brainstorm
around what the team's passionate vision is.
Make a Wordle or word cloud capturing the main words.
A day later, ask the individual team members to email
their vision in a Tweet format.
Pair your co-workers anonymously and
ask them to comment on the vision of the other.
Provide this feedback to the owner of the vision.
A week later, get everyone together and
ask the pairs (whose identities you now reveal) to sit
together in small groups to discuss their visions and
feedback received.
Turn the ideas into a maximum of five great visuals!

ꜰꜰꜰꜰ ꜰꜰꜰꜰ ꜰꜰ ꜰꜰꜰꜰꜰꜰ ꜰꜰꜰꜰꜰꜰꜰꜰꜰꜰꜰꜰꜰꜰꜰꜰꜰꜰꜰ

TO RECAP, HERE ARE THE FOUR KEY CHARACTERISTICS OF AGILE ORGANISING:

- **SMALL, AUTONOMOUS TEAMS**
- **LIMITED NUMBER OF BASIC DECISION-MAKING PRINCIPLES**
- **LOOSELY COUPLED STRUCTURES**
- **A PASSIONATE VISION**

The organisational cancer of the past: positional organising

While a lot of small start-ups easily radiate the above characteristics, established organisations tend to encounter hurdles in making the agile shift. One of the big hurdles is what is called *positional organising*.

During the 1960s and 1970s, fast growing organisations needed management experts to professionalise their functional domains. Because reward mechanisms in those days (and perhaps still today in your organisation) were based on measuring how managers performed within their silos, managers started building fiefdoms. For years, these fiefdoms competed against each other to become the most important, deserving of the highest rewards, and to deliver the next CEO.

This 'positional' form of organising led to managers guarding and exploiting turf and wasting massive amounts of time ensuring that their interests were secured, whatever the cost. Because of the slow pace of innovation in the past, organisations had the 'luxury' of tolerating power games and even bearing the cost. Today you can no longer afford that kind of waste. In times when speed and co-creation for innovation are necessities, positional organising is like a deadly cancer. Because power games make you inward-looking and divert your attention from what's happening in your environment, you slow down your ability to respond quickly to change!

EVALUATE THE COMPOSITION OF YOUR PROJECT TEAM

Team members are probably invited into the team
to represent their departments, right?
Everyone probably genuinely believes
that this diversity will lead to great, innovative solutions
because all 'stakeholders' are considered in composing
the team.
But let's be honest, the only thing anyone is doing there
is defending their own turf.
They say to themselves: 'Everything can change,
as long it has no or little impact on me or my department'.

Our advice is: for each key project, compose teams with
people from diverse functional areas
who are eager to passionately contribute to a great
solution for the benefit of the whole value chain.
The more creative they are, the better!

The still dominant mindset of 'internal competition leads to higher performance, which leads to higher profit', is misleading – in *soaring* environments, knowledge sharing is key to speeding up and co-creating.

> '**P**ower exists – as it always has –
> in providing people with dreams.'
> —Ridderstråle & Nordström[24]

What a pity that all your highly paid specialists are constrained by status quarrels and turf battles. What a pity that their expensive brainpower is employed to play these games... games that leave winners, losers and, ultimately, victims. Acting from self-interest in the long term does not serve the greater good of the organisation and society. On the contrary, it leads to bankruptcy! Both rooting *and* soaring will profit from getting rid of power mongers, or at least 'power mongering'.

It should come as no surprise that enlightened organisations are slowly but surely eliminating these power games. They understand that if organisations want to be really innovative, organising is not about what you create within your unit – it is about *the impact you have on the whole value chain.*

Managers of links, not of things

What is the most important component of a car? What is the most important element of your organisation? We hope your answer is: 'There is no such thing as the most important part. The strength is always the quality of the connections between the parts.'

All decisions that you make as a leader, have consequences both within and outside of the organisation. Your responsibility lies in creating levers for the many next links in the value chain, not in maximising the strength of your own link. Agile organisations are conscious of their ripple effects. They focus on value creation processes for the long term, in other words 'expanding value', rather than simply generating short-term shareholder value.[25]

That's why we need to ban positional power. Great leaders at all times imagine and evaluate how their decisions impact on others. Leaders must become the masters of the 'ripple effect'.

Leaders are the consequence of their actions, they are not their intentions. What matters in life is the impact they have on their environment and on others. Therefore, organisational reward systems should be based on the *long-term impact leaders and their decisions have*, not on the good intentions behind their decisions.

TRY THE PRE-MORTEM TEST

To understand the ripple effect of your decisions more clearly, we suggest you occasionally try this useful tool:
Before implementing any decision, imagine that your ideas or plans have failed.
This goes beyond looking at threats and risks.
Map the intended and unintended consequences.
Then conduct a brainstorming session where you map the reasons for this 'failure' and
fix the gaps before hitting the 'go' button.[26]

Here's an everyday example.
The best car Herman had ever driven was a Toyota Avensis.
Yet, when he needed to replace a broken headlight, he could not do so himself, despite being rather handy with these things, because part of the engine was in the way.
He had no option but to have the light replaced by a garage.
This probably was not the intention of the designer,
yet for Herman this design had expensive consequences.

A sustainable solution =
a solution that creates a ripple effect that
adds value for all who are affected by it.

Agile leaders are skilful at foreseeing the possible ripple effects of what they do, because they are 'intimate' with the 'moments of truth' of their organisations. Moments of truth are those moments when the organisation's products or services are consumed by others. It is the end result, the final 'ripple' of the leader's and their team's efforts that counts. In traditional management, the distance between decision makers and these moments of truth is often huge, because the focus is inwards, not outwards. This is not surprising as the silo and hierarchical structures of traditional organisations create a false image of the reality beyond the silos.

MASTERING THE RIPPLE EFFECT

The Master was walking through the fields when a young man,
a troubled look upon his face, approached him.
'On such a beautiful day, it must be difficult to stay so serious,'
the Master said.
'A beautiful day?' the young man said, for his mind was
elsewhere,
and he felt he had the bad luck of the whole world.
'Join me if you like,' the Master said.
The Master walked to the edge of a still pond.
'Please, sit down and find a small stone,'
the Master invited the troubled young man.
'What? A stone?'
'Yes, and please throw it in the pond.'
Searching around him, the young man grabbed a pebble and
threw it as far as he could.
'Tell me what you see,' the Master instructed.
Straining his eyes to not miss a single detail,
the man looked at the water's surface. 'I see ripples.'

'Where did the ripples come from?'
'From the pebble I threw in the pond, Master.'
'Please reach your hand into the water and stop the ripples,'
the Master asked.

The young man stuck his hand in the water as a ripple neared,
only to cause more ripples.
He was now completely baffled. Where was this going? Had he
made a mistake in seeking out the Master?
Puzzled, the young man wailed.
'Were you able to stop the ripples with your hands?'
the Master asked.
'No, of course not.'
'Could you have stopped the ripples, then?'
'No, Master. I told you I only caused more ripples.'
'What if you had stopped the pebble from entering the
water to begin with?'
The Master smiled such a beautiful smile,
that the young man could not be upset.

'The next time you feel unhappy,
catch the stone before it hits the water.
Do not spend time trying to undo what you have done.'

Whatever we do or say has consequences.
So, think before you act, listen before you speak.
Ponder the possible ripple effect of your actions and words.
While we cannot always predict how our words or deeds will
affect others or our society,
we should always ask what the consequences might be
of what we are about to do or say.

Author unknown[27]

Integrated data systems: a necessity

Agile organising needs integrated data systems for improving decision making and mapping the ripple effect.

Integrated decision making (IDM) is about getting access to and connecting the best existing, real-time and relevant information provided by all stakeholders throughout the value chain. This 'big data' can provide accurate information beyond silos, thereby 'linking' them and making the impact of local decisions crystal clear: so no home-based Excel spreadsheets per unit, but one overarching smart system. In building this smart system, you may need to make a 180° mental flip: integrated information should be available to all co-workers; it should not only enable the higher levels in the organisation to tell others what to do. Smart systems replace this part of the job of management and make some of its interventions barely necessary. Impact becomes visible thanks to the smart system, which provides continuous feedback allowing for real-time adaptation.

While rooting and soaring will profit from IDM, soaring needs 'orchestrating' as well. Orchestrating goes on top of IDM: it brings the best ideas from the internal and external ecosystem together in a co-creation process leading to either innovative or disruptive products and services.[28] Losing time because of silo-based decision making is just clearing the path for your competitors.

Useful slack: deliberate inefficiency pays off

THE EINSTEIN ROOM

A CEO tells us: 'Every three years and for six months at a time, we give our employees the opportunity to spend their Fridays in the company's "Einstein" room with colleagues from other departments. They work together around a self-chosen work-related project. Management is not even aware of what they are working on. Great ideas and implementations come out of this.'

What were you thinking when you read about this practice? Were you preoccupied by thoughts of costs and inefficiency, or whether your HR policies would permit this? Or did you find yourself thinking that a lot of needless training (about employee motivation, innovation, or coping with burnout) could be avoided by installing this kind of practice, a practice that could have real impact?

We are not the first to underline the importance of creating settings where co-workers can experiment with new ideas and new collaboration formats; in other words, where they can safely soar and practice agile thinking.[29] We also know that these settings are to some extent 'deliberately inefficient' in terms of a rooting logic. That's why we call such a practice 'creating useful slack'.

You are not able to soar if you are stuck in the rut of the track, frequently the consequence of lean management. Although never its intention, lean management frequently takes away innovativeness from within. Our mind closes down when we are under excessive stress brought on by multiple priorities to cope with; when we suffer from several change processes taking place simultaneously; when we get bombarded by a tsunami of email and social media messages; when we are in the middle of turbulent personal and social lives; when we experience information overload. Stress forces us into survival mode, where there is no room for either creativity or innovation.

The more turbulence they experience, the more your co-workers (and you) need useful slack, not only to recharge batteries, but also to create a peaceful frame of mind that allows the exploration of new ideas.[30]

To deal in an innovative way with the unexpected, agile organisations create 'slack resources' that allow them to deal with the unforeseen.

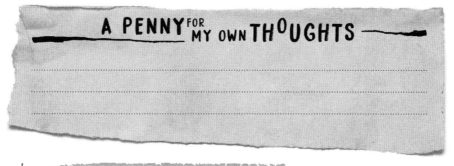

A PENNY FOR MY OWN THOUGHTS

....

....

....

A CONCEITED MAN AND THE MOTH

A conceited man found a cocoon of an emperor moth.
He took it home so that he could watch the moth
come out of the cocoon.
That afternoon a small opening appeared.
The conceited man watched the moth as it struggled to force
its body through that little hole.

Then it seemed to stop making any progress.
It appeared as if it had gotten as far as it could and it could go
no farther. It just seemed to be stuck.

The self-centred man lost his patience.
He decided to force the situation and help the moth.
He took a pair of scissors and snipped off
the remaining bit of the cocoon.
The moth then emerged easily.
But it had a swollen body and small, shrivelled wings.

The man continued to watch the moth because he expected
that, at any moment, the wings would enlarge and expand to
be able to support the body, which would contract in time.
Neither happened!

In fact, the little moth spent the rest of its life
crawling around with a swollen body and
shrivelled body and wings.
It never was able to fly.

What the big-headed man in his haste did not
understand was that
the struggle required for the moth
to get through the tiny opening,
was the way of forcing fluid from the body of the moth into its
wings so that it would be ready for flight once it achieved its
freedom from the cocoon.
Freedom and flight would only come after the struggle.
By forcing his approach upon the moth, he deprived the moth
of a healthy existence.

Author unknown[31]

A waste of money?

Slower is faster in a VUCA world

In a VUCA world you need to go slow, to move fast. Intrigued? Then we recommend that you read (or perhaps reread) John Kay's book *Obliquity*.[32]

Let us illustrate the 'go slow, to move fast' idea with a well-known example. To protect national parks from fires, the traditional response was to install a lot of observation posts so that fires could be spotted and action be taken immediately. Seems logical, doesn't it? Yes, but putting out fires rapidly causes a lot of dead wood to accumulate over time (wood that would otherwise have burned). Sooner or later, a thunderstorm will pass by and, when lightning strikes, it will cause what is known as a 'hot' fire, which burns underground and damages seeds and roots of plants and trees. It can take years before nature recovers. 'Cold' fires – that burn dry material only – occur regularly and naturally in nature to ensure that long-term damage to the environment is limited.[33]

Having a 'cold' fire from time to time, even if it looks inefficient, can prevent worse things from happening. Losing billable hours, even if it looks inefficient, can produce creative ideas that sow the seeds of innovation and future success!

Go on a blind DATE:
DAre to Trust and Empower

By now you've developed your *strange attractor* (your passionate vision). You've *loosely coupled* your teams (project organisation). You allow *useful slack* and will soon provide your team with *simple decision-making rules* to guide their endeavours (see part 4). You've also reminded them to be *mindful of their ripple effect*. It is time to be daring and to empower your team!

Employee empowerment is a key requirement when you want to soar. *Those who are nearest to the moments of truth should lead the dance*: close connection with clients throughout the value chain provides real-time information for quick adaptation and innovation. No time is lost with internal checks and balances, the need for hierarchical approval processes, or watchdogs of specialised internal control mechanisms. Imagine what a cost saving *not* having all those controls could be!

LOOKING INSIDE FOR SOLUTIONS

Most companies trust external consultants more than their own carefully recruited and expensive personnel! But are external parties really more in tune with your organisation's challenges? Do they have better real-time information than those at the frontline? Are home-grown solutions necessarily inferior?

There can only be two explanations for trusting externals more: either your co-workers are not competent enough, or the politicking within your organisation makes fast and transparent feedback impossible. As a consequence, it becomes 'safer' to work with the external advisors, leaving your co-workers disempowered. But what a double cost if this is the reason for looking outside!

'**R**eplace the traditional management adagio of "trust but verify", with "trusting you is my decision; proving me right is your choice".'
—Anonymous[34]

The faster you can gather and share honest information about what is going right and what is going wrong, the sooner you can adapt to what's happening. To openly share or receive information you need a climate of trust, where people feel psychologically safe and are allowed to fail wisely, learn from it and share the lessons learned with others. Empowerment and trust go hand in hand.

Naturally, you shouldn't be naive and trust blindly: you trust because the other is trustworthy and trustworthiness flows from competence, consistency and credibility. Lack of trust, however, causes politicking, in-fighting and fear of the consequences of disclosing bad news to decision makers. As a result, opportunities for making quick adjustments collaboratively, based on authentic, real-time information, are missed.

If someone trusts us, we score: those who trust us tend to want to collaborate with us and provide us with exactly the kind of information we need to enhance our decision making.[35] Here's what we mean...

Rehabilitating the ugly duckling

Within a rooting context, one of the old prescriptions of good management is to make all processes in your organisation explicit and formal so that you can master and control them. Yet it is naïve to think that all information can be formally captured, and if you only rely on the informal data you will become slow to adapt! You need to recognise and nurture the so-called 'informal' organisation to be truly nimble.

The informal part of any organisation is frequently seen as the proverbial ugly duckling, a kind of underground movement arising from the psycho-dynamics between co-workers trying to find the gaps and 'profit' from the system by making their own tasks easier. Because it appears to be subversive, managers often want to nip such informal activities in the bud.

Yet, in the fairy tale, the ugly duckling turned out to be not so ugly after all! Imagine I could study the operational manual of a nuclear plant by heart in a couple of days. Would you trust me to be responsible for the safety of the plant, despite having no experience? Hopefully not! I lack the experience to apply the rules in a flexible way when the situation calls for it.

Rules may provide good solutions 80% of the time, but for the remaining 20% we need something in addition to them: the *collective informal knowledge and experience* of those doing the work, which often go way beyond what the rule book says or requires.

This informal knowledge makes things work within a context. You compensate for the rigidity of the rules, you create new practices in response to new external demands. It's the informal organisation that ensures that the work finally gets done. Yet this resource is usually driven underground and remains unspoken. If your co-workers are made to fear non-compliance with the rules and therefore don't use their ingenuity to solve unique problems that the rules don't foresee, or to simplify processes in a way that the rules don't provide for, rigidity sets in.

Remember, most control and auditing systems have one big objective: finding and penalising those who disregard formal instructions.

Have you ever arrived at an airport when the customs officers were on a work-to-rule strike? Did this slow down or speed up the process? How pleased were you as a traveller?

The informal organisation contains the seeds of innovation through the 'connectedness' it creates between co-workers, who are the real implementers. They are the ones who live the 'moments of truth'. They know what works, what doesn't, and how to find a workable solution, even if the route to the solution is not always 'by the book'.

Far from representing a threat to their authority, the informal organisation presents leaders with a dynamic resource that is better able to adapt to the demands of a turbulent environment. Formal and informal can and must coexist: they are dizygotic twins, the one as important as the other.

Make sure the unspoken becomes spoken!

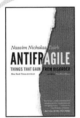

IN TRYING TO CREATE STABILITY, WE RISK TO MAKE THE ORGANISATION FRAGILE

'Too much formal process can be harmful, in the way that it eliminates the chance for the organisation to prove its self-organising ability. Organisations and managers underestimate the natural antifragility and the power of self-organisation.'
- Nassim N. Taleb[36]

This is where so-called change agents are sometimes oh-so wrong: in trying to create stability they build for fragility instead of creating 'antifragile' systems, ones that are resilient in the face of turbulence.

Challenge your thinking !

Question 1

* *Think of a recent important decision you took. Map the ripple effect of your decision: How did it affect others inside and outside the organisation? Is the impact desired and sustainable? Should you change anything?*

Question 2

* *Have all your co-workers and even your clients bought into the vision of your company with equal passion?*

* *Or is it merely shallow window dressing? If so, becoming agile may be almost impossible.*

Question 3

* *What stops you from creating some useful slack to set up your own Einstein room?*

Make your choice, stay where you are OR TAKE THE LEAP !

Everyone suffers from 'meeting overload'.
Yet it is only fair and democratic to involve
the different departments,
and by doing so respect their territory,
even if this slows us down.

OR

We create settings where our best people,
driven by a passionate professional vision,
voluntarily seek out co-creation
opportunities.
When it comes to the operational decisions,
well, we trust our experts and smart
systems!

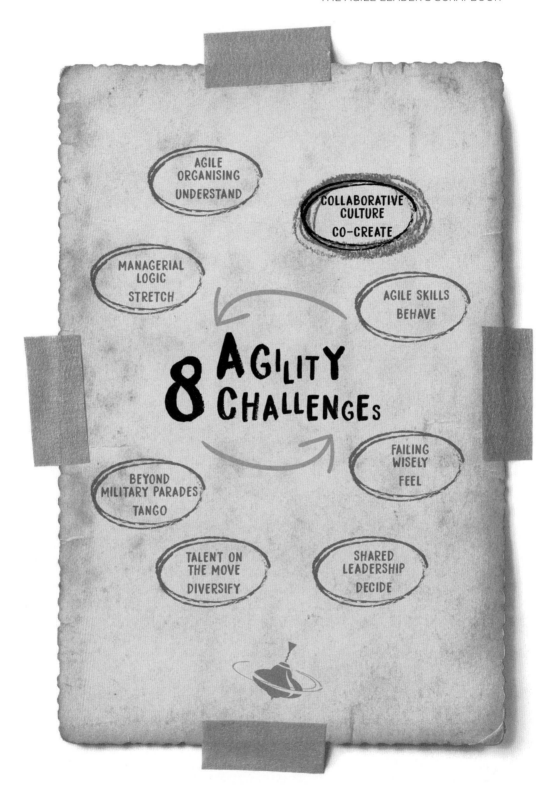

AGILITY 3
CHALLENGE

In need of a **COLLABORATIVE** culture

Organisational agility will forever remain elusive if you lack the necessary cultural climate and accompanying agility skillset. Here we challenge you to think about the *readiness of your organisational culture to become agile*. In part 4 we look at the kind of skills you and your team need to be able to take off and soar.

Meetings are like traffic jams

As Picasso once said, every act of creation implies an initial act of destruction. First to go should be the unnecessary, boring, time-consuming, often unproductive and therefore costly meetings your organisation has on a daily, weekly or monthly basis. We all know that most of them have nothing to do with real co-creation.

As meetings often prove, bringing co-workers together is one thing, getting mileage out of their collaboration is quite another! In terms of costs (number of people in meetings * salary cost * quality of decisions taken * commitment), meetings are probably one of the most wasteful and inefficient investments you make, often without any tangible return.

Why are meetings generally so boring and unproductive? Well, because the bulk of meeting time is spent sharing information about operational issues, information that could be provided by integrated data systems. And if space and time *are* created for co-creation in meetings, most of those leading the meetings lack the necessary skills to really employ the enormous potential and brainpower of participants. How we run meetings is a major cause of underperformance by an organisation and its people.

Not convinced? Let's illustrate our point with three examples of bad meeting practices:

THE BOSS ALWAYS SPEAKS FIRST!

Fine, as long as the boss explains the decision-making process to be followed. Most of the time, however, it sounds more like this: 'I think the problem is ..., and probably the best solution is ..., but if you think there is another way, please comment ....' The boss frames the context and the problem *and* also indicates the road to resolution (and sometimes the solution itself)! By doing so, the boss dampens the participants' critical faculties. Called the 'sunflower bias', this is the tendency for everyone to follow the boss's ideas, suggestions and opinions.

Bernhard Günther (CFO of German electric utility RWE) explains the danger of this: 'Depending on the way you organise decision processes, when the boss speaks up first, the likelihood that anybody who's not the boss will speak up with a dissenting opinion is much lower than if you, for example, have a conscious rule that the bigwigs in the hierarchy are the ones to speak up last.'[37]

The combination of a boss having first say and the inevitable hierarchical power inhibits most participants and wastes their time! Participants' voices are silenced and key contributions they could make in terms of unique information and solutions, are lost.

Take a look and enjoy:
www.youtube.com/watch?v=aioN3k8N0nE

② PLAYING THE YES-BUT GAME!

You know the story: one participant launches an idea which then becomes the focus of a yes-but discussion: someone will criticise the idea and the meeting quickly becomes polarised. Meeting time is taken up by playing verbal tennis, in other words. At the end of the meeting, the chair sums it up with: 'Well, I think that the majority seconds person A's solution, so let's go for that.'

This severely limits the creative brainpower of the group to a binary, 'either or' discussion around *one* alternative. Does anyone really believe that, because the majority finds person A's argument more persuasive, those views must be right? Innovative ideas often come from the minority! Instead, actively encourage dissension, debate and brainstorming of *multiple* ideas and alternatives. As we suggest later on, using 'yes, and' or 'no, but' is far more productive if you want to stimulate creative thinking.

③ THE BORING 'TOUR-DE-TABLE'!

A (too) large group of participants are invited to take turns to explain their activities. The chairperson comments, opens the floor to questions, and then moves to the next person. In the meantime, everyone else is busy checking emails, updating their virtual networks, or drifting into boredom. In the case of virtual meetings, this lack of engagement becomes worse! Only those who are the focus of the chairperson's attention are active. For the rest, brains collectively fall asleep.

Get rid of that old-fashioned meeting style

If you aim to become more effective in co-creation and agile decision making, it is time to throw your traditional meeting practices overboard. Start by aggressively reducing the number of meetings you have by at least 40%. If the meeting is intended only for information exchange, it probably shouldn't be held in the first place – the information can be distributed electronically. Rest assured that it will come as a big relief to all but the most stubborn.

JUST GO FOR IT

Replace meetings with regular digital team updates – there's enough software and technology around to help you out with this. Make sure someone takes up the responsibility to bring the most diverse information together in an informative and creative way. Use icons to indicate what type of information can be found in your communication. Since the ripple effect is so incredibly important, focus as much as you can on the impact of events, information or trends throughout, across and beyond the organisation. Interactive software will allow you to get comments, extra ideas, likes or dislikes to make this information dynamic. You can always have a brief online session for those who still have questions.

If you have a culture of spreading certain project meetings over a long period (e.g. meeting each Monday morning for a whole year about a project), reconsider whether this is optimal. This approach tends to slow things down, is static and encourages politicking. Rather invest several days in a row in the project!

Last but not least, when it comes to rooting your organisation, entrust your specialists with more decision-making power regarding matters falling within their expertise and accept the decisions they take. Don't bring those decisions to a meeting (under the cover of democracy), unless it's truly necessary. It only consumes valuable time. Rather free up this time for innovative work and find other ways to keep people informed about what the specialists are busy with!

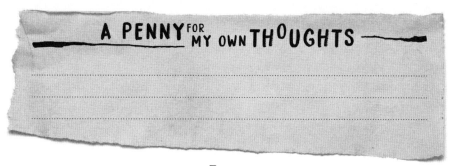

A PENNYFOR **MY OWN THOUGHTS**

Just about everything you've ever read or learnt about how to run a meeting can go in the dustbin.

The future is co-creation

Merely reducing your meeting load is not enough. You have to replace them with something that is more efficient and innovative: welcome to the co-creation process!

Every organisation needs to assign specific tasks and roles to its people – that's nothing new. Yet if specialists are locked up in their silos, unaware of what others are up to, or criticising what others do while fighting for their own turf, no value is added. 1+1 will not even equal 2. The aim of soaring is to ensure that the whole is greater than the sum of its parts. For this, co-creation across silos, hierarchies and fiefdoms is absolutely necessary.

Get mileage out of the clash of brains and skills of those co-workers who eagerly want to innovate for tomorrow.

This is your objective and the very meaning of co-creation. It is a process that allows people with different skills and different points of view, who belong to different parts of the value chain, to provide positive energy to (re)define business challenges and work collaboratively to develop and implement innovative solutions.

These days, your competitors have access to the same sources of information and knowledge that you do. But your co-workers become the winners if they are able to process and combine this knowledge quickly and in advanced ways. Train and coach your specialists in co-creation skills, not to turn them into generalists, but to create a 3 out of 1+1!

Ask yourself: 'How can we, together, create an improved product or service that creates the ripple effects we want in line with our values and mission and the needs of our customers?'

Co-creation asks of people who may never have cooperated to create something together that none of them can create single-handedly. It is about positively and actively wanting and acting in unity with others to achieve a common goal.[38] This presents both a mindset and a skills challenge.

Developing a collaborative space

Society – and the business world – in general still operates very much in a competitive mode and mindset when faced with challenges. We want to 'kill the competition'; wage 'wars on talent'; be 'number one', and so on, while the challenge today is to co-create to *expand value*. To paraphrase Nigel Nicholson: we did well to leave behind the Stone Age; the only problem is that the Stone Age hasn't left us.[39]

While competitive behaviour is appropriate in certain contexts (e.g. playing a game or a sport, vying for a job), it becomes a problem when we are required to co-create.

The 'collaborative' organisation of today is one where people are structurally encouraged to work with others internally across hierarchies and silos, and externally with customers, suppliers and, sometimes, even competitors. Collaboration is not about getting everyone to think and behave the same way. It is about inviting and orchestrating differences of opinion and diversity until unique ideas and solutions emerge – what Quick and Feldman refer to as 'inclusive' practices.[40]

Cultivating a collaborative mindset throughout the organisation is one of the leader's biggest challenges; after all, it goes against our instinctive 'fight or flight' responses when others disagree with us, or hold different views or challenge ours. Creating the right conditions for this is key. What, then, are the characteristics of a collaborative culture? Three stand out for us.

(1.) IF YOU LOVE THEM SET THEM FREE

A 2016 doctoral study concluded that employees who are made accountable for *how* they do their work (not the output as such) are considerably more willing to search for new and better ways of doing things.[41] This kind of insight should make you question the current set-up of your teams and organisation, as well as aspects like your recruitment and selection criteria.

Following the fractal logic we referred to in part 2, the secret lies in creating flexible structures to facilitate cross-team and cross-functional collaborations while dispersing the ability to make decisions. Silos are replaced with modular units that freely engage, exchange information and ideas, and recombine according to the needs of the moment. Agility requires an emphasis on decentralising decision making as far as possible, combined with continuous high-speed learning.

If you are thinking that this is a recipe for free-for-all chaos, or that anyone can decide on anything, no, that's not what we mean. Your co-workers' decision-making powers are focused on that which is within their scope of responsibility. Their decision-making 'freedom' is also guided by a set of objectives, your organisation's vision and agile decision-making principles and is supported by coaching from your team leaders or managers (see part 4).

② LEADERS SHOULD BE SPACE CREATORS

'Master, what are condor pairs thinking when their youngsters leave the nest?' asked a couple, while drinking *sake* with the old wise man in front of his cave.

The Master looked out over the valley and answered with a smile: 'Nothing, really nothing. They're not thinking at all. They look upon their young hopefully and marvel at how they dive and spread their wings. And even though their own bodies instinctively follow the twists and turns, they let their young fly on their own. This is the moment the condor pair has been longing for. "Fly, soar to your own heights," they screech, while enjoying the spectacle of their young soaring on the wings of their happiness.'

'But Master, don't they give their children anything?' asked the concerned couple.

'Not what you might think. Gifts would only burden their flight. The condor parents have already given them the most important thing of all: the gift of time... time to look at the reality, to dream and to make plans to make a difference in the great valley below. Time to learn from failed attempts at flying. Time to enjoy what they do and one day, to pass their joy on to others.'

'Master, please tell us: what then remains for the condor pair?' insisted the couple.

'Look at the sky and look at the valley... the enormous space in which their offspring will find their own way. To share the space side by side is in itself a dream. Occasionally their flight paths will cross and they will share their adventures. They are there when they need to be. They let go when they have to. And that is the great secret of continuing to soar in each other's presence.'
The couple drank their sake together until late in the evening, silently learning more about the flight of the condors.

Herman Van den Broeck

Leaders become architects, designers and enablers of co-creation. They then trust their co-workers to produce the desired outcomes. To use an analogy: on the battlefield, those at the forefront of the battle need to make decisions on the go and cannot wait for instructions from fight command for every manoeuvre. The command structure provides the principles and parameters of the decision-making authority of those on the frontline and equips them with the skills and tools to make those decisions.

Leaders have to start feeling comfortable with letting go of the need for tight control and get used to models that are loose and flexible enough to allow for bottom-up, self-organised, goal-oriented activity to emerge. Achieving agility and innovation lies in self-organisation.

While it is often believed that the key to this kind of cooperation is technology, it is in fact a culture of co-creation, information sharing and contestation that is definitive. The skillset of the future will have to include a collaborative approach to problem solving, decision making, and resolution of tensions and conflicts.

(3.) COACH MORE, MANAGE LESS

Managing involves authority, telling, directing, and specifying results to be achieved. It is directive and (mostly, short-term) task oriented. It works well when there's a crisis and a quick decision needs to be taken, or when someone lacks the experience or skill to do what is required. Coaching, on the other hand, involves exploring, facilitating, taking into account many possible outcomes and a long-term focus. It is developmental.

In an agile organisation, leaders manage when required, but mostly act as coaches. They focus on and appreciate the talents in their team, challenge them, inspire them and guide them. They don't 'crack the whip' or merely tell people what to do and how to do it; they instead provide opportunities for exploration and learning. They set objectives and provide autonomy to their team in terms of how to achieve those objectives.

Let's turn now to the specific skills your organisation needs to make agile decision making a reality.

A PENNY FOR MY OWN THOUGHTS

Challenge your thinking !

Question 1

✳ *Are you one of those domineering power mongers around the meeting table who likes to force their views upon others?*

✳ *When you kill the ideas of others, you give them permission to do the same to you.*

Question 2

✳ *Do you agree with Garry Hamel when he suggests that, 'instead (of) moving decisions up to where people have competence, you move competence down to where people have real-time information and they can make good decisions'?[42]*

✳ *What does this imply for your organisation?*

Question 3

✳ *Are you and your peers stuck in your silos?*

✳ *Do you still compete for status and recognition of your ideas and contributions?*

✳ *If so, don't be surprised to find resistance to co-create, for it rises like yeast!*

Make your choice,

stay where you are

OR TAKE THE LEAP !

The gap between what's formally declared
and what happens in reality is huge.
There is no feedback culture,
but rather a gossip culture.
Competitive mindsets and behaviours
stymie collaboration and innovation.

OR

Every co-worker has a 'voice'
and may express it.
Their views are sought and appreciated;
we know they are the seeds of improvement.
'Speak up to solve' is our mantra.

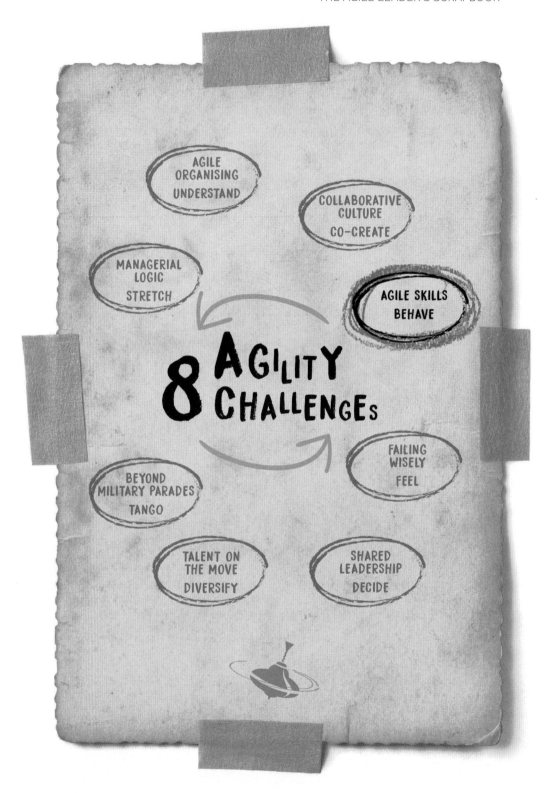

AGILITY CHALLENGE 4

Skills CLUSTERS for soaring

An agile culture and mindset require a supporting skillset that enables co-creation and fast, sound decision making. In part 2 we explained how the interaction between fractals is guided by only a limited number of rules. Let's start, then, with a limited set of principles which will help your organisation to behave like a murmuration (such as an enormous flock of birds swooping through the sky without colliding) during decision-making processes.[43]

Decision-making principles for soaring[44]

Don't tell your co-workers what to do! Rather train and empower them on how to take autonomous decisions. Here's our list of key principles for agile decision making (ADM):

- Visualise what the ideal future would look like – you will find the 'why?' there!
- Always apply backwards thinking: work from the desired future to where you are now.
- Focus on optimising the whole and not solely the individual parts.
- Always have a range of different scenarios or options to choose from.
- Build on each other's ideas using the 'yes, and' technique.
- Nobody owns an idea, ideas belong to all!
- Key opportunities deserve 'useful slack' to enable appropriate dedication to them.
- Bring competencies around the table, not representatives of competing silos.
- Especially involve those with a professional desire to be innovative.
- Use integrated data, but also listen to seasoned people's judgment and intuition.
- Suspend your belief that 'there is no other way'. There is always another way, and if you don't discover it, your competitors will!
- Finally, build a bridge between rooting and soaring.

Make sure these key principles for ADM are known, and embedded in the organisation through training and reinforcement. This will help you to trust the ability of your co-workers to autonomously make sound decisions.

Apart from these principles, agile organisations also need collaborative environments that encourage diversity, autonomy, flexibility, risk taking, failing wisely and an intense flow of explicit and implicit knowledge, on which co-creation thrives.[45] We identify three clusters of skills to achieve collaborative environments.

Three critical skillsets

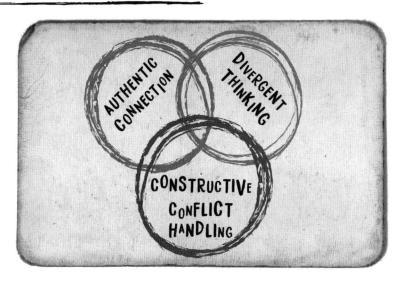

CLUSTER 1
AUTHENTIC CONNECTION

This means that debate and the exchange of information between co-workers and units are as open as possible. There is *authentic connection* when co-workers and units are eager to learn the points of view of others to broaden the collective mindset.

> 'When managers genuinely value relationships in the workplace, and truly listen to people and act on their suggestions, a culture of care and connection emerges in which people are highly responsive to the needs of the organisation. Teams can form spontaneously and powerfully in this context, and the job gets done.'[46]

Organisations have three 'faces', each of them with a unique purpose.[47] As well as the *formal organisation* (the first face), there is the *informal organisation* (the second face). As we explained in part 2, the informal organisation contains all kinds of knowledge, thinking and behaviour regarding how individuals and teams adapt the formal rules and procedures to today's reality on a real-time basis. The implicit knowledge of the informal organisation makes the formal rules workable and allows the organisation to deal with new opportunities and challenges in an agile way. In traditional environments, this is often perceived as contrary to policy and worthy of sanction; in truly agile environments, it is regarded as the seed of innovation. The third face is the *façade*: the way your company presents itself to the outside world.

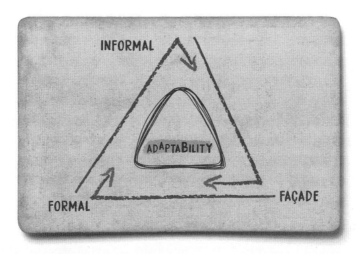

In an agile organisation, to create authentic connections inside and outside the organisation, people use the gaps between the three 'faces' to enhance learning. Only the best available information will allow you to be fast, innovative and able to adjust quickly when you need to. When we say information, we are not only talking about rules and procedures, or quantitative ratios delivered by integrated data systems – that is a mind stuck in rooting mode. If you have access only to this kind of formal information, your decision making will be crippled whether you are rooting or soaring.

Instead we urge you to mobilise all three kinds of information and especially the 'gaps' (inconsistencies) between them. Are your team members allowed to voice their thoughts and observations about the gaps between what is expected, what is really happening and what is presented to the outside world? Do you encourage them to speak up about this? And when they do, do you jump into defensive mode, or do you start a collective learning journey?

CLUSTER 2
DIVERGENT THINKING

A clear shift from the emphasis on convergent thinking (looking for the single solution) towards divergent thinking (exploring many possible solutions) is needed. Identifying the ways in which we limit our thinking and actively seeking ways to go beyond these limits is crucial. Ideation comprises all stages of the problem-solving cycle, from problem definition, to generating multiple ideas, to planning for implementation. In each phase, identifying the right question is the most important and difficult part. Identify the key questions first, before jumping to solutions. Again, your motto should be: slow down to speed up!

CLUSTER 3
CONSTRUCTIVE CONFLICT HANDLING

Autonomy goes hand in hand with weak power structures and a culture of constructive conflict handling and dissent.[48] Encouraging a diversity of views can create tensions and conflicts, but these shouldn't limit creativity; on the contrary, if managed well, they should enrich the decision-making process. Conflicts have the potential to be sources of positive energy and innovative outcomes.

Where differences arise – and they will – the important thing is to focus on the *issues* and not the personalities – separate the people from the problem.[49] It has been said that oysters and conflict have something in common: 'a little irritation can produce a thing of beauty'.[50] Dealing with differences in a collaborative, side-by-side manner can bring fresh insights, strengthen relationships and build trust. Solve the conflict now, because hiding and avoiding it will only increase passive resistance and office politics.

Co-workers therefore have to learn to become comfortable with conflicts, sometimes even encouraging 'loud debate'. Authentic connection will ensure that these conflicts don't become 'relational' issues.

Organisations will also become more 'conflict wise' if they actively encourage diversity of views, ideas and insights. Internal contradictions have been referred to as the engines that are 'responsible for the creativity and dynamism of our species'.[51] Accepting contradictions is key to constructive growth. A globalised world offers a lot of contradictions, too, and we should want to learn from, and not fight, them!

You may be wondering: but how do agile organisations tolerant of conflicts get this right? Well, let us provide you with a few ideas to implement across your organisation and with a lasting ripple effect.

HOW TO? Cluster 1: Authentic connection

Active talking versus active listening

How many of your colleagues love to hear themselves talking? Do you? This common propensity is not only due to ego; it's also because, when we are over-stressed, we cannot stand the silence that listening to others requires. But without really hearing the ideas, motivations and needs of others effective co-creation is impossible!

How can you hope to ever change their minds if you have no idea what's on their minds?

We communicate to be heard, but to be heard, leaders need to hear others first. According to the *principle of reciprocity*, we earn 'communication credits': I heard you, so now you need to do the same for me. We are prone to selective hearing, yet listening actively provides us with new information and gives us insight into the frame of reference of the other, into what they find important. In other words, the other person gives us a great gift, the gift of having alternatives to our (subjective) perspectives.

Listening has other benefits too. It has psychological value because it satisfies a deep-seated human need to be heard or acknowledged. Listening gives people 'voice', contributes to the open climate needed for agility and enhanced employee involvement, and creates 'social capital'.

YOU PROBABLY KNEW THIS, BUT DO YOU PRACTISE IT? HONESTLY? HOW MANY TIMES IN A DIFFICULT CONVERSATION HAVE YOU SUSPENDED YOUR VIEWS AND JUDGMENTS AND INSTEAD ASKED QUESTIONS TO UNDERSTAND THE OTHER PERSON'S THINKING? HOW OFTEN HAVE YOU TRIED TO UNDERSTAND THE OTHER BEFORE DEMANDING THEY TRY TO UNDERSTAND YOU? DO YOU LEAD BY EXAMPLE? DO YOU PROMOTE A LISTENING CULTURE IN YOUR ORGANISATION?

Become obsessive about 'Yes, and'!

The difference between average and outstanding collaboration is that the latter avoids the tyranny of 'either or' thinking and instead embraces the genius of 'yes, and'.[52] 'Yes, and' means you explicitly make clear how you value the idea of the other and then enrich this idea by adding other possibilities aligned with it.

You can also try 'no, but' – it indicates what is not acceptable to you, yet shows that you are willing to seek alternatives. 'Yes, and' and 'no, but' should become stock phrases in co-creation sessions instead of conversation killers like 'yes, but' or simply 'no!'

The 'yes, and' and 'no, but' mentality allows us to leverage and constructively face tensions. Rather than choosing one option or view at the expense of another, this approach generates novel ideas containing both elements. It must be clear that a 'yes, and' or 'no, but' optimises your decision-making abilities! Are you a 'yes, but' person'? It's time to stop setting a poor example. And do challenge the people in your organisation to make 'yes, and' and 'no, but' part of their daily lexicon!

Give 'voice' to all

Organisations are full of power mongers who surround themselves with people who are inclined to subserviently say 'yes' to everything they do or want.

THE LION WITH BAD BREATH

The Lion was in a bad mood. That morning his wife, the Lioness, had told him that his breath smelled, and that perhaps he needed to do something about it. The Lion had pretended not to care, and had roared loudly and angrily just to show the Lioness who was king. Secretly though, he was worried.

So as soon as the Lioness left the den to go about her day's work, the Lion called his three counsellors: the Sheep, the Wolf and the Fox.

First, he called the Sheep. 'Tell me, Sheep,' growled the Lion, 'do you think my breath smells?'

The Sheep thought the Lion wanted to know the truth. So she bowed low before the Lion and said, 'Your Majesty, your breath smells terrible. In fact, it smells so bad that it is making me feel quite ill.'

This was not what the Lion had wanted to hear. Roaring angrily, and calling the Sheep a fool, he pounced on her and bit her head off.

Then he called the Wolf. 'Tell me, Wolf,' growled the Lion, sharpening his claws, 'do you think my breath smells?'

The Wolf had seen the dead Sheep on the way, and he had no plans to end up the same way. He bowed low before the Lion and said, 'Your Majesty! How can you ask me that? Your breath smells as sweet as the flowers in spring, as fresh as the...'
He could not finish what he was going to say. 'Liar!' roared the Lion, and ripped him to pieces.
At last the Lion called the Fox. The Fox came warily; she had seen the dead Sheep and the dead Wolf on the way.
'Tell me, Fox,' growled the Lion, sharpening his claws and yawning widely so that the Fox could see his long sharp teeth, 'do you think my breath smells?'
The Fox coughed and sneezed and blew her nose, and then clearing her throat noisily, said in a hoarse whisper, 'Your Majesty, forgive me. I have such a nasty cold that I cannot smell a thing!'

Aesop[53]

The antidote to this kind of abuse of power is to give people 'voice' – all co-workers are both encouraged and allowed to speak up, without fear of being ridiculed, blamed, shamed or penalised for doing so. Giving employees voice – allowing them an opportunity to be heard – is intimately connected to the generation of organisational trust.[54] Research confirms that having voice '... builds trust and commitment, ... produces voluntary cooperation, and voluntary cooperation drives performance, leading people to go beyond the call of duty by sharing their knowledge and applying their creativity. In all the management contexts we've studied, whatever the task, we have consistently observed this dynamic at work'.[55]

Collaborative teams need the best information they can get to enhance their decision-making. If people are not encouraged to share their ideas, or are afraid of negative consequences if they do, they will keep their mouths shut and you will make decisions based on incomplete data!

Especially when tackling contentious issues, leaders who are good at engagement give everyone a voice but not necessarily a vote.[56] For your own sake, allow all opinions to surface. Give co-workers 'voice': executives should talk less and ask more questions.[57]

If you beat a gecko long enough, it will tell you it is a crocodile. But what's the value of the information you receive?

Invite and welcome unique information

Giving people 'voice' gives you access to real and sometimes contradictory information from those at the frontline of production or the customer interface. You shouldn't search merely for confirmation of your ideas. Listen for the unique perspectives of others. What everyone thinks and agrees with is probably the least innovative. For how else will you be able to break out of your mental boxes? Can you see other's perspectives as a gift of alternatives, and not as a threat to your status? Only an unfettered exchange of insights and ideas can build a comprehensive understanding of the environment and generate appropriate adaptations and innovative solutions.[58]

'De-bureaucratise' your organisation by systematically reducing the volume of formal rules, policies and procedures and updating those that remain by taking heed of your organisation's implicit knowledge.

Don't present an idea (even a co-created one) to others as a fait accompli

People will almost instinctively resist and feel alienated. We all want to feel autonomous, to have choices – not to be told *not* to think for ourselves. Leaving people without a choice kills their desire to creatively contribute.

HOW TO? Cluster 2: Divergent thinking

Arm yourself, build your 'peripheral vision'

The most valuable information for innovation often comes from the edges of our vision. That's why agile entities have frontal *and* peripheral vision. They are attuned to signals of change from the internal and the external environment. They have the ability to decode signals and to quickly respond to new information in appropriate ways. On top of that, they know that that which cannot be predicted can often be discovered through experimentation. Here are some ideas to strengthen your peripheral vision:

Continuously vary your information sources between different print and electronic media as well as the regularity of your news consumption. For example, read financial or specialist journals for a few weeks and then switch to in-depth news articles online. Read good books on leadership, disruption and how digitisation will impact sectors other than yours.

Build your 'scan-squad' network. Network with people who are open-minded, who are attuned to what happens outside your company (and not only with your clients) and who can, with vivid imagination, translate this information into great opportunities inside. Talk to those who appear to have stories – even strange ones – to tell. This can be people who are hooked on the latest management trends; someone who recently followed an interesting external training event; people working in a completely different sector but from whom you might learn something; or those who are very active on social media. Give them the spotlight. Let them talk in meetings about what they found surprising or useful.

Regularly look for and throw out fresh challenges to yourself and your co-workers: 'Why are we doing things this way? Is there a better way?' If the answer eludes you, it's time to revisit the why, the what and the how of what you are doing, with the 'why' being the most critical!

Do something completely new and startling on a regular basis. Never been to the opera? Well, there you go! How about an exposition of modern art, or a heavy metal concert? How about a visit to an exhibition of new technology or a trade show? A visit to a great ancient culture? Or a strenuous nature trail? Do this with one big question in your mind: What can I learn from this?

Connect intensely with the moments of truth within your company. How else will you grasp the impact of the ripple effects of your organisation? Sometimes those lower down in the hierarchy know much more about an issue; make sure that their low status does not cause them to be ignored.

Never criticise or block ideas that seem stupid

Remember the rules of a good brainstorming session: generate before you evaluate. Above all, know that stupid-sounding ideas are often attempts to solve an intelligently defined problem and will associatively lead to the solution. Also, taken on its own, the idea might sound stupid, yet it might become intelligible if evaluated along with other options in the mix. Often you will end up combining them. This is an excellent moment to practise your new 'yes, and' attitude!

Never decide what to eat without having seen all possible dishes on the menu or asked about the specials of the day!

Don't demand that 'everyone should pull in the same direction'

Never ever start a meeting where you want to encourage divergent thinking with a statement like this. People will feel afraid to come up with fresh ideas. Remember that while soaring, it is uniqueness you need to go for.

Never ever start your decision making with an 'as is' evaluation (status quo-ism)

You don't want to reinforce the association your team members have with the past, you want them to uncouple from it. Again, making an as-is analysis is very useful in the rooting zone, because you want to improve the 'what is'. But when soaring, you should start with a 'let's dream' session to visualise the great future you want to create.

A mini brainstorm as an easy start

To activate people's creative capacities, ask your team to individually write down three suggestions to a problem, issue or idea before you start the session. Write these up and ask for further suggestions. Then start evaluating the options using decision-making criteria. Don't make the person who launched the idea speak first, as this will start the positional game all over again. Nobody owns any of the ideas expressed – they belong to the group. The big challenge is to enrich and build on each idea.

Share half-baked ideas as quickly as possible

When you operate with an agile logic, you must be able to share from the very beginning even 'half-baked ideas' with team members and units to get direct and quick feedback about whether they are worth exploring further. For an analytical mind, it might seem dangerous and not professional, yet having direct and real-time feedback from more links of the value chain will help to leverage everyone's contribution, to speed up and so shape a better outcome.

Bring the 'collective default mindset' to the surface

A famous quote attributed to, amongst others Anaïs Nin, says that 'we don't see things as *they* are; we see things as *we* are.'[59]

The outputs you generate, the decisions you make, are highly influenced by your own and the collective default mindset (mental models and assumptions). Some are still perfectly suitable, and very helpful. Others become obsolete because of changes in the environment and function as 'false knowns', limiting your ability to adapt quickly.

False knowns are firmly held assumptions that are at the same time questionable. Take the example of Gillette: in an attempt to be innovative, they simply added extra blades to their non-electric shavers despite consumer preference changing in favour of electric shavers. For them, innovation meant doing more of the same, just better.

Kodak is another example. Its business model was based on the assumption that people bought film to take photographs. In reality, people mainly bought film to capture memories to keep and share. This became evident when the likes of Facebook, Snapchat and Instagram became so successful. Kodak's old model is history. Airbnb realised that many travellers and holidaymakers need variety and flexibility beyond what hotel chains typically offer. Today it is the largest 'hotel' group on the planet. Airbnb understood that there was perhaps a shortage of hotel rooms, but not a shortage of rooms! Can you too test and reframe some of your assumptions?

The danger with starting from an outdated mindset, is that we become impervious to the changing context and end up putting more energy and resources into what seems to be working for the moment. And who can blame us... if it's not broken, don't try to fix it! In the 'old' world, this type of thinking worked most of the time. In the 'new' world, it is dangerous.

To be able to be innovative, you should become conscious of your default assumptions so that you can work at overcoming them. List the *dominant knowns*, but also the *underexploited knowns* (mega trends you may recognise and perhaps even have acted on but without sufficient speed or emphasis). Last, but not least, try to identify the *unknown unknowns* (intrinsic uncertainties that you can prepare for only by hedging your bets).[60]

A PENNY FOR MY OWN THOUGHTS

Regularly reconfigure your teams

Given how instinctive 'herd' mentality is, it can happen very quickly if you're not careful. Don't let the same people always work together. Split and mix them up so that they can experience different group dynamics and gain fresh insights. An alternative is to put them in different roles; for example:

- give some the role of answering why the ripple effects of a pending decision or idea could be negative, while others focus on why the ripple effects will be great;
- let some take on the role of the ultimate internal decision maker to whom an idea or solution has to be sold, while others play the role of clients, unions, or other co-workers;
- let some take a short-term perspective of the impact of what it is you are deciding to do, while others take a medium- and a long-term perspective.

Make sure you do not consult the same people all the time, as they might just begin telling you what you want to hear instead of what you should know!

Look at the mavericks

Shift the focus from what your traditional competitors are doing to what new players are doing. If you really want to be innovative, remember that best practices are often useless; they only push you towards the average standard. This is perhaps useful while rooting, but when you need to soar, you'll only end up in places your competitors have already been.

Break free and become empowered…
Start thinking how and where
you can be disruptive!

Select a flexible team format

There are many team formats to choose from, such as war, skunk, scrum teams, and so on. Start experimenting with them and get your HR partners to help you with this.

Why are teams like this so good at delivering the desired output? The reason is quite simple: they are given and take the time to deal with their top priorities in an engaged and focused way. They don't have a multitude of priorities, or bosses who intervene with bureaucratic demands, only the desire to succeed. Wherever possible, these team formats ensure face-to-face (not necessarily in person) contact, trusting and relying upon the competencies of each other to get into flow.

Flexible team formats allow teams to focus fully. They are not chained to the bureaucracy of the rest of the organisation, but work autonomously. They are more agile and prepared for innovative solutions because they have eyes, ears and feet on the ground as well as a broader view. They are at the coalface of the problems that they encounter and therefore can make quick decisions without having to constantly refer to the hierarchy. This is quite different from the usual parade of employees who drag themselves daily towards their silos, doing the same thing over and over again in accordance with the rules and instructions passed down from above.

Make sure every team member
gets proper training in creative
thinking technique!

HOW TO? Cluster 3: Constructively dealing
with differences

Speak out or leave the stage

All levels of the organisation have to demonstrate a genuine commitment
to seek out and listen to ideas from across the organisation, irrespective of
hierarchy. Leadership must create safe spaces where people feel at liberty
to raise concerns, initiate new ideas and even respectfully challenge what
those higher up in the organisation propose without fear of reprisal or
marginalisation.[61] This will only happen if people have a sense of psychological safety at work.

Yet people also need to understand that *not* speaking up is not fair either:
their ideas might benefit others, while their silence might lead to poor
decisions.

Ask people to speak out.
Refrain from actions that silence
contrary views.

Appoint devil's advocates

It is the explicit role of the devil's advocate to challenge and be contrary!
Make sure everyone understands and appreciates this role. The best devil's
advocates are respectful of others, listen well, and, because they are also

critical in their thinking, make others *think* too. This may invite conflict, but who else will be the catalyst for you taking the leap out of your mental box? As Polman says: 'We must find and create tensions – force people into different spaces for thinking... This is not just a performance issue but a survival issue, because managing paradox helps foster creativity and high performance.'[62]

Within an old meeting culture, too many leaders seek approval for solutions already decided on. When you are on a constant mission to reinvent yourself, you have to work with people who are prepared and encouraged to challenge you.

You probably have enough yes-men and yes-women around you. Why are they still there?

Don't search for others to blame

Conflicts trigger our emotions. Our neural networks go into defensive mode and so we quickly try to shift the blame onto someone else to protect our self-image. The sad thing is, once we have identified the 'guilty' ones, we stop thinking further and learning. Be mature enough to know that *you* might be part of the problem. It is up to you to be part of the solution. Don't simply accuse others of having bad intentions; rather discuss the impact of what they do or did by focusing on the facts.

Review after some time

Especially with key decisions, agree on a moment to reflect on and evaluate how things are going. If necessary, adjust. In that way, you show commitment to implement the solution and you feel psychologically committed too. You need fast feedback to be able to adjust fast!

Empowered teams as organisational devil's advocates

Thanks to their *loosely coupled status*, empowered teams have the ability to question the overall dominant managerial logic: 'Networks become a necessary part of successful organisations – directly, or in association, allowing them to test, interpret, and develop the rules and truths embedded within them.'[63] If organisations don't allow and empower these critical units, they become stultified.

Bye-bye SMART, hello CONDOR

In the rooting space, it is quite okay to be guided by buzz terms such as 'SMART' ('specific, measurable, achievable, relevant, time-related'). But when you need to soar, these terms can create thinking hurdles. Here's our own buzz term for the agile era: 'CONDOR'.

Collaborative mindset   to co-create

Open climate   to speak the unspoken

Never 'yes, but'; always 'yes, and'   to find solutions

Dance with diversity   to go beyond the status quo

Overcome your comfort zone   to dare to discover new horizons

Recognise the ripple effects   to assess your real impact

Having read the first four parts of this book, you should understand this new mantra. You are now ready to soar on the wings of your own strengths.

Challenge your thinking !

Question 1

✳ *Are you a 'yes, and' person?*

✳ *Can you challenge yourself to apply this technique in meetings and even during conflicts?*

Question 2

✳ *How long has it been since one of your colleagues came to you with bad news that could impact your decisions?*

✳ *Have you in the meantime taken important decisions without really knowing what was going on?*
How can you ensure a better flow of information from those who might know more than you?

Question 3

✳ *Do you recognise some of the following default mindsets?*
'Online sales is not for us'; 'we have to benchmark our activities'; 'our clients will never pay for that'; 'we are selling commodities'; 'as a not-for-profit organisation we cannot do this'; 'the same HR rules should be followed by and rooters and soarers'.

✳ *How can you reframe these kinds of statements and find fresh answers?*

Make your choice, stay where you are OR TAKE THE LEAP!

Failure is not an option and
management makes that clear to everyone.
Our bonus system rewards
those who are profit and loss driven
and ensures they increase their
turnover every quarter.

OR

Cleverly experimenting new ideas is
encouraged, which also means that
mistakes can be made –
as long as we learn from them
and share the valuable insights acquired.

The art of **FAILING** wisely

'**F**ailure should be our teacher,
not our undertaker.
Failure is delay, not defeat.
It is a temporary detour, not a dead end.'
—Denis Waitley[64]

There are times when you need to hold the reigns tight to steer your horse in the direction you want to go. Yet when you want to enjoy the exhilaration of a horse at full gallop, you need to gently let go. In this case, the unexpected can happen and the horse might stumble.

People are no different: tighten the reins and they will do exactly what you tell them to do and no more. If you want them to be entrepreneurial and innovative, if you want them to take the responsibility to learn and to adjust, you have *to free the reins and allow them to make mistakes*. You will reap the rewards.

'**Y**ou don't learn to walk by following rules. You learn by doing, and by falling over.'
— Richard Branson[65]

Learning, however, cannot take place without feedback. Yet if you want people to soar, you'll have to reinvent the way you support, coach, mentor and evaluate them. Annual performance reviews are a thing of the past. Long live continuous feedback!

The habit of continuously reflecting on work experiences and providing and asking for feedback boosts learning significantly. Important questions to ask include: 'What turned out differently to what I expected?' and 'What have I learnt from this experience?' Leaders who demonstrate and encourage reflection not only learn more themselves, they also 'spur increased contextual awareness and reflective practice in others, thereby laying a foundation for higher levels of learning agility in their teams and organisations'.[66]

So, the lesson is: free the reins! By doing so, you show people that you trust them. This earns you social capital (trust) and unleashes your team's creative potential. By allowing for and requiring regular feedback, you also limit your risks as you are able to keep a handle on things.

Instil a growth mindset

We cannot emphasise enough how important it is for agile organisations to create a culture within that allows for experimentation, failure, feedback and collective learning.

Accepting the fact that there is always room for improvement, talking honestly about our failures, sharing lessons and receiving feedback from peers, teach us to turn the 'how not to' into a 'how to'.[67] As a consequence, we develop a 'growth mindset' which allows us to feel, think and act differently in meeting the challenges ahead. Instead of focusing on impossibilities, we actively start looking for new possibilities to make the best out of every situation. The more people realise that failure, and learning from failure, are highly valued, the more likely they are to want to soar into unchartered territory.

Individuals and organisations lacking a growth mindset tend to play the blame game when mistakes are made. Unless someone did something unethical or committed a serious misconduct, it shouldn't really matter who 'initiated' the mistake. It certainly isn't worth throwing the proverbial book at them. The focus should be on what everyone in the organisation can learn from it. Failure is an *organisational event*, not a person!

Seven key characteristics of a growth mindset

Here we share the seven main *attitudinal* characteristics of people and environments nurturing a growth mindset.

(1.) ENCOURAGE EXPERIMENTATION

Experimentation is a core process in discovering innovative ideas, products and services. The time when companies invested in that one great idea is over! This is far too risky in an uncertain world! Agile companies support and rely on continuous strategic experimentation and always have multiple options to play with.

> '**I**'ve missed more than
> 9000 shots in my career.
> I've lost almost 300 games.
> 26 times, I've been trusted to take
> the game-winning shot and missed.
> I've failed over and over and
> over again in my life.
> And that is why I succeed.'
> —Michael Jordan[68]

(2.) CELEBRATE FAILURE

Experimentation invites failure. It should come as no surprise therefore that leading agile organisations accept this as normal and use it as an opportunity for collective learning. They encourage co-workers to not only share their successes, but also to share their failures for everyone to learn from. In fact, they go further: they see making mistakes while trying something new as a cause for celebration, as it shows that someone is not walking the well-trodden paths, but exploring new ones.

Life is not about whether or not one makes mistakes – mistakes are a given. It is about how fast you can learn from the mistakes you make. This is what 'failing wisely' is about. To paraphrase Meyer, while it is often believed that the key to an agile organisation is technology, it is in fact the culture of failing wisely that is definitive.[69]

Within most organisations talking about failure is not the done thing. It might even reduce your status and that of your team or department if you 'owned up' to your mistakes. Yet hiding this information ultimately makes decision-making processes less efficient. A growth mindset, on the other hand, allows you to critically reflect both on what's going well and what isn't. In this way, you can improve on the quality of decision-making in the future. You should welcome the tension between what you planned for and what really happened as the pre-eminent source of learning. So, go beyond the misleading focus only on celebrating success because it prevents you from learning.

③ FEELING COMFORTABLE WITH FEELING UNCOMFORTABLE

As humans, we suffer from 'status quo-ism': we prefer stability and keeping things as they are. Change therefore makes us feel uneasy, even more so when we are the ones who are required to change. Changing our habits and mental models – an essential step towards agility – takes us out of our comfort zone and might even shake our self-confidence. Yet that's usually a good sign, because it proves that we've learnt something new! Giving up old routines and ways of thinking is always a struggle. All you can do, is keep practising the new insights and behaviours until they develop into an improved, comfortable routine.

'If you want to feel secure, do what you
already know how to do.
But if you want to grow ... go to the cutting
edge of your competence, which means a
temporary loss of security.
So, whenever you don't quite know what
you are doing,
know that you are growing.'
—David Viscott[70]

④ OVERCOMING THE FEAR OF FAILURE

At school, we received lower grades if we made mistakes. We rarely got praised if we learnt from these mistakes. In organisations, we are frequently punished by the established reward and performance systems if we make mistakes.

A growth mindset abhors this kind of thinking. When assessing people's performance, we should be able to determine how good an employee was at learning from and sharing their mistakes and reward them for it. Kenney invites us to 'create an environment inside the organisation where employees feel the psychological and practical safety to collaborate and pursue new ideas – an "intellectual safe harbour" in which unfamiliar perspectives and approaches are expected and encouraged in response to, or anticipation of, unfamiliar circumstances'.[71] This is the way to go if you want your co-workers to overcome their fear of failure.

⑤ TAKING INTO ACCOUNT SINGLE AND DOUBLE LOOP LEARNING

A company that wants to create a growth mindset helps individuals to practise both 'single loop learning' and 'double loop learning'. The former involves improving the established goals and rules, whereas the second involves changing the system in which the established rules are embedded.

For example, a salesperson who has lost a client might say: 'Yes, I was responsible for this client, so how can I improve my client relationships?' (single loop learning). But she will also reflect on how the entire sales system, which provides her with information, should change to be able to better meet the client's needs (double loop learning).

While a lot of team-building initiatives do bring team members closer together (single loop learning), learning will not deepen if reward systems remain unchanged and continue to value competitive behaviour higher than collaboration. Nothing changed at a double loop level, in other words. As a consequence, we have a dichotomy between what was learnt during the training and the reality back at the office. This only leads to more frustration in the organisation.

UPSTREAM ACTION

A group of people are standing at a river bank and suddenly hear the heart-breaking cries of a baby. Shocked, they see an infant floating – drowning – in the water. One person immediately dives in to rescue the child. But a few seconds later, yet another baby comes floating down the river, and then another, and another! People continue to jump in to save the babies and then see that one person has started to walk away from the group who was still on shore. Accusingly they shout: 'Where are you going?' The person's response is as clear as crystal: 'I'm going upstream to stop whoever's throwing babies into the river!'

Author unknown[72]

6. TAKING THE TIME TO TRY OUT AND PRACTISE NEW WAYS

It is one thing to learn a new approach, yet quite another to make it stick and to apply it. Without time to practise it, we may continue to make the same mistakes over and over again, never really changing our mindset or behaviour. In other words, never really growing.

Running around like a headless chicken trying to do it all in one short working day, is not a good idea either. You may think your output is great – but it's often quite the contrary! Cognitive overload depletes the ability to think clearly and be truly productive. Give your people some 'useful slack' to experiment... and grant yourself that privilege as well.

Do you have time at work to learn and practise new things? Are you allowed to set aside some time so that you can try and master a new competence or explore a new idea? Do you have the time to reflect on and try out things you've learnt during a recent team building or corporate training session, so that the company gets a return on that investment? If you are a leader, do you give others some 'useful slack'?

'Our Ancestors were graced
with an abundance so that
they had time to carve,
time to sing, time to dance,
and time to beautify the things
they made and did.'
—'Ksan Museum, Hazelton, Canada

7. THE PROCESS OF 'MUDDLING THROUGH'

The decision-making models we read about in scholarly works are almost always straightforward rational, linear models. These models typically involve a four-step process: *define the problem – seek alternatives – choose a solution – develop an action plan.*

From a theoretical standpoint, this might seem optimal, yet most decision processes do not work like that. Sometimes we start with a current solution, only to discover that others have alternatives in mind, turning us back to the question of what we truly want to solve, to finally (and often by coincidence) stumbling on a new technology that provides the solution. As far as we are concerned, this does not have to have a negative connotation. In fact, most decision-making processes alternate between linear progress and iterative moments.[73]

'By seeking and blundering we learn.'
—Charles E. Lindblom [74]

You shouldn't believe that people are merely or always rational creatures, nor should you discount the seemingly irrational part of decision making. Instead use it to improve the outcomes of your co-creation meetings.

We suggest you experiment with just 'muddling through' to get to a decision. Although it seems a waste of energy at first glance, it will offer you the flexibility you need to deal with your VUCA environment. Start with low-impact decisions, those with limited risks attached to them. To muddle through, make use of the following questions, in any order you like. You'll find that the decision develops organically through this process.

A PENNY FOR MY OWN THOUGHTS

QUESTIONS TO SUPPORT 'MUDDLING THROUGH'

What are the real needs and expectations of our clients (old and new)?

Have we defined and 're-framed' the challenge at hand?

Why is this an issue or problem?

Where does our 'how-we-did-it-until-now' thinking contribute to the problem?

What are our current overt and hidden assumptions? Are they still valid?

Is a 'more-of-the-same' approach to solve the challenge the best way?

If not, what are the alternatives?

Building resilience: learning to cope with mistakes[75]

In highly politicised environments one can find a lot of 'quiet fixers'. These people have learnt to quietly correct their mistakes because of the risk that these mistakes (and even the adaptations they come up with) will damage their careers, is real. In such organisations failure is not an option; as a consequence, neither is fast learning.

Hiding mistakes does not improve individual or organisational learning! Real learning is about sharing your insights, enhancing your professionalism and expertise, and trying to turn failures into improvements that you, your colleagues and clients can profit from.

This being said, the following characteristics can help foster a growth culture.

Self-confidence to experiment and grow

People with self-confidence are comfortable with pushing their boundaries, accept that they are not perfect, and are prepared to risk making mistakes so that they can learn from them. People with low self-confidence, on the other hand, often feel the need to defend themselves for everything they think, say and do, because they perceive the slightest negative feedback as an attack on their person.

If there is one priority for you as an employee, manager or leader, it is to find the 'sweet spot' in your current position: where you feel confident to thrive on the competences you do have, and where you are able to develop your strengths through experimentation, trial and error. From there you can spread your wings and grow.

> **'F**ailure happens. Give people trust and it will happen more productively.'
> —Ridderstråle & Nordström[76]

A belief that mistakes can be an opportunity to learn and grow

People who see mistakes as irrevocable failures either feel depressed when they make a mistake and give up trying out new things, or blame others. Neither reaction is helpful: they amount to failing 'un-wisely'. No learning can take place without experimentation, making mistakes and learning from these mistakes. Perceive your mistakes as an essential part of the learning curve you are on. Develop a *sense of agency*: in other words, do something about it instead of merely moaning about it!

 ### *Discovering and addressing the root causes of our mistakes*

It is quite an art to emotionally disconnect from the awkward feelings one experiences on discovering a mistake. The key is to distinguish between the *visible consequences* and the *root cause* of the problem. If you've just realised that you provided the wrong advice to a customer, for example, take time to reflect on how this happened – how did the context or external factors contribute ('double loop learning') and how did you personally contribute to this 'mistake' ('single loop learning')? Maybe you were under too much pressure or perhaps a situation at home distracted your attention (the context). Few of us are completely immune to what psychologists call the 'fundamental attribution error' – a mindset or internalised belief whereby we tend to attribute the causes of a mistake to external factors. For example, after losing a football game you might conclude: 'We lost the match because the referee was against us'. The upshot is that there's nothing for you to learn as it's someone else's fault, in this case the referee's. Instead you should ask yourself: 'How did I contribute to this?', 'What can I do differently next time?' and 'How can I help change the context?'

 ### *Masters in unlearning*

Those who fail wisely are 'able to let go of perspectives or approaches that are no longer useful – in other words, they can unlearn things when novel solutions are required'.[77] Many individuals and organisations suffer from what is known as 'learned helplessness'. The routines that were established in the past conveniently provide automatic answers to the new problems confronting us. They block our willingness and our ability to adapt. Driving a car while constantly looking in the rear-view mirror won't help you avoid the obstacles ahead! If the challenge you face is routine and your past solutions tended to deliver good results, by all means continue to use those 'rooted' and stable approaches. However, if the challenge is new, you need to keep your eye on the road more often than you look to the rear. Or rather, you need to have peripheral vision to see the obstacles coming from the front and the sides.

Routines are not all bad; by saving energy they give you the space to conquer new horizons.

Humility: learning to apologise

Mistakes can have consequences ('ripple effects') that you might never have intended. Be humble enough to own up to your mistakes, to share the experience so others can also learn from it. Also take responsibility for stopping the 'ripple' by tendering an apology or expression of regret for the mistake you made. This will create a constructive collaboration culture, where others will be much more willing to own up themselves and help each other avoid what can be avoided and fix what went awry.

Keeping promises

To be sure that you are trustworthy, you should not only 'talk' about your mistake and about what you have learned from it, but you should also *change* your *behaviour*. Make this new behaviour visible and ask those who were affected for feedback about whether they experience added value.

Of course, the reason for our mistakes might have little or nothing to do with a lack of information, fear of failure, and so on. It might simply be the result of the influence of decision-making biases, something all of us are subject to. To fail *wisely*, we need to be acutely aware of these biases.

Be aware of your decision-making biases

We are not as rational as we might think we are. Research shows that we all overestimate the quality of our decision-making skills.[78] One famous example of common thinking errors that led to a major disaster was the decision by NASA officials to launch the Challenger space shuttle despite evidence being available that cold temperatures were likely to cause failure of a crucial engine part. The so-called investment bias (all the efforts made and costs incurred to ensure a successful launch) coupled with groupthink (resulting in critical voices being ignored) led to very bad decision making. All seven astronauts on board died when the vessel exploded shortly after lift-off as a result of failure of the particular engine part.[79]

Having an ego is not necessarily bad; being led by it is courting disaster.

When making important decisions, the minimum requirement is access to smart data systems to aid your decision making. What are important decisions? Those that will have a big ripple effect – a long-term impact for you, others, the organisation or society, or that may have a big financial or moral impact.

Different techniques exist for countering our biases. For example, you could ask a neutral party to actively challenge your thinking and conclusions before finalising your decision. Another technique is that used by German electricity utility RWE, which makes it mandatory for decision makers to list the de-biasing techniques that were applied as part of any major proposal that is put before the board.[80]

While we cannot escape these biases – we can only be conscious of them – below is our checklist for countering their effect.[81]

CHECKLIST FOR COUNTERING THINKING BIASES

✳ Are you giving too much weight to recent anecdotal evidence?

✳ Is the information too good to be true (too easy to believe)?

✳ Are you stuck on personal ideas, habits, solutions?

✳ If you were the initiator of the idea, do you feel you need to push it further to not lose face?

✳ Was the first piece of information so convincing that you didn't bother to look for alternatives?

✳ Did you ask only for confirmation of your ideas and ignore the critical voices?

✳ Did intense emotions get in the way of your decision making?

✳ Have you decided to do it, because others are doing it?

✳ Do you and your team show signs of over-confidence, perhaps even some contempt for others' views?

IF YOU ANSWER AFFIRMATIVELY TO ANY OF THESE QUESTIONS, RE-EVALUATE YOUR DECISION!

Challenge your thinking !

Question 1

＊ Do you have practices in place to celebrate failure and which allow for collective learning?

＊ Do people in your organisation get punished or rewarded for failing wisely?

Question 2

＊ Are you aware of the differences between single and double loop learning?

＊ Do you apply double loop learning to understand and address recurring problems?

Question 3

＊ Are you a quiet fixer?

＊ What would happen if you spoke to your boss about a problem you are dealing with and have been quietly trying to fix?

＊ Do you encourage and empower your co-workers not to be quiet fixers?

Make your choice, stay where you are OR TAKE THE LEAP!

Working and surviving in an organisation
characterised by bureaucratic
control systems that straitjacket your
creativity and the brainpower
you were hired for.

OR

Working and thriving in an organisation
where you are empowered to be creative
and entrepreneurial and where
high levels of trust stimulate you to
grasp the opportunities you see.

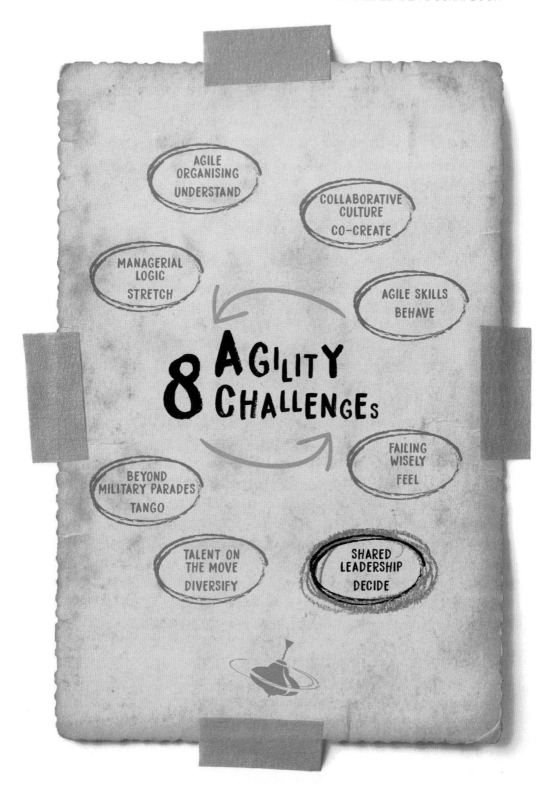

AGILITY CHALLENGE 6

Towards shared LEADERSHIP

'The greatest danger in times of turbulence is not the turbulence. It is to act with yesterday's logic.'

—Peter Drucker[82]

The antidote to the turbulence, it has been said, is leadership with Vision, Understanding, Clarity and Agility (VUCA reversed).[83] A far more attractive and empowering state, isn't it? Before we become more specific about shared leadership, let's start with explaining what leadership in an agile context should *not* look like.

Conquering our Stone Age mindset

While today's organisations require leaders who empower those they lead to soar, most leaders of today earned their stripes serving a rooting mindset. What's more, many of these leaders saw their careers blossom thanks to the scope they had for exerting hierarchical power and control to protect their fiefdoms, further encouraged by various reward systems.[84] Blaming the systems would be misleading, however. Research indicates that those who get to the top have a neural and hormonal network programmed to win – and in winning they want to see others lose.[85]

To be able to soar, organisations need leaders who can subordinate their own ego and agenda ('humility') and give up personal power and self-interest, and who are willing to share organisational resources for the sake of the greater good. Leadership should not be about imposing one's ideas on others, but about empowering others.

This is easier said than done, of course. Looking at typical leadership profiles, we can hardly be blamed for wondering whether promoting collaboration beyond the silo (the modern 'cave') is counter-intuitive to homo sapiens. Yet one of our biggest distinctions as a species is also our unique capacity to make counter-evolutionary choices.[86] This includes the ability to adapt our mental models or mindsets from *competition* to *collaboration*.

In his excellent book *Sapiens*, Yuval N. Harari reasons that living beings, to be able to survive and cooperate in large groups, need an imagined order.[87] An imagined order consists of a number of implicit and explicit agreements (beliefs and norms) to regulate cooperation. It is not natural laws (e.g. the law of gravity) that steer us towards cooperation, says Harari, but shared imagined realities. Homo sapiens has the ability to create such an imagined order, the very reason we are at the top of the food chain. Organisational hierarchies are also 'imagined orders'. If we have the skill and competence to create one imagined order, we should also have the competence to re-create it!

Most of us dream of a world in which people are able to constructively deal with differences and live peacefully alongside each other. Yet, notwithstanding this shared longing, testosterone-driven leadership often results in destructive competition against anyone deemed to be even a vague threat to our interests or egos. Selfishness, greed and a lack of maturity to recognise that another's order can be a useful order as well, seem to be the cancers of nearly all imagined orders. They are the main drivers behind the destructive conflicts that exhaust today's world, exhausting our species and the true 'natural order'.

Today, due to globalisation, the intensively connected global community is confronted more than ever with the challenge of finding constructive answers to the tensions between the many variations of imagined orders that exist within. Instead of fighting such orders, however, this 'richness' of alternatives should stimulate us over and over again to challenge and, if necessary, redefine our own individual and communal order. Can the human race constructively redefine its imagined orders into something more focused on working together towards a common good? Indeed, just as nature can bring in a new order through destruction, it is also capable of doing so in constructive ways. Just as organisations can kill the human spirit through endless and unnecessary competition, so can they create environments – orders – that spawn collaboration, innovation and creativity. It is *leadership* that makes the difference.

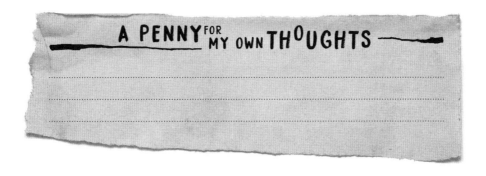

A PENNY FOR MY OWN THOUGHTS

A leader should create space and opportunities for soaring

Leadership is not about one person controlling others and imposing decisions on them. True leadership is about creating an environment that allows innovative solutions to develop from the best ideas available and getting those involved to take collective responsibility for the decisions they make. As such, the collective also becomes *responsible* for the output and the impact of their decisions (their 'ripple effect'). Scholars refer to this as 'shared leadership'.

Shared leadership is focused on safeguarding the co-creation process and on guiding or facilitating outcomes, rather than directing them. It is about leading the process, not telling people what to do. It is about making connections, bridging diverse competencies and mindsets, and getting people to share and create ideas and resources across hierarchies and silos.[88] It is about minimising the use of blunt power that only serves oneself.

IMAGINE A WHEEL

To commemorate a glorious victory in war, the Emperor had invited high-ranking military and political officials, poets and teachers to a grand celebration. Among them was Chen Cen, the master to whom the emperor had often gone for enlightenment during his campaign to unify China. A banquet, grander than any had ever seen, was held. At the centre table sat the emperor with his three heads of staff. At another table sat Chen Cen and his followers.

While food was served, speeches given, honours presented and entertainment enjoyed, Chen Cen's three followers remarked: 'Master, all is grand, all is befitting, but at the heart of the celebration lays one enigma.' Sensing their hesitation, the Master gently encouraged them to continue.

'At the central table sits Xiao He. His knowledge of logistics cannot be refuted. Under his administration, the soldiers have always been well fed and properly armed. Next to him, Han Xin. His military tactics are beyond reproach. He understands exactly where to ambush the enemy, when to advance and when to retreat. Last is Chang Yang. He sees the dynamics of political and diplomatic relations in his palm. He knows which states to form alliances with, how to gain political favours and how to corner heads of state into surrendering without battle. What we cannot comprehend is the centrepiece of the table, the Emperor himself. He cannot claim noble birth, and his knowledge of logistics, fighting and diplomacy does not equal that of his heads of staff. How is it, then, that he is emperor?'

The Master smiled. He asked his followers to imagine the wheel of a chariot. 'What determines the strength of a wheel in carrying a chariot forward?' he asked.

After a moment of reflection, his followers responded: 'Is it not the sturdiness of the spokes, Master?'

'But then, why is it,' he re-joined, 'that two wheels made of identical spokes differ in strength?'

After a moment, the Master continued, 'See beyond what is seen. Never forget that a wheel is made not only of spokes, but also of the space between the spokes. Sturdy spokes poorly placed by the craftsman make a weak wheel. Whether their full potential is realised depends on the harmony between them; think now, who is the craftsman here?'

Author unknown[89]

SHARED LEADERSHIP LEADS TO FASTER AND BETTER DECISIONS. WHY IS THIS?

First, because decision making does not take place in a vacuum.[90] Co-workers and key stakeholders are part of the process from the very beginning; they continuously provide the necessary information and feedback and feel psychologically committed to see the process through. So, decisions taken at the top are not isolated from reality but are connected with what really happens in the workplace.

Second, the availability of integrated data ('smart systems') enhances the understanding of the potential impact of what the collective decides and does. One of the keys to agility is smart information. The best organisations distinguish themselves by the way they gather and process information to harness 'collective intelligence'. As Couzin explains: 'Interactions with others can enable individuals to circumvent their own cognitive limitations, giving them access to context-dependent and spatially and temporally integrated information. This can result in more accurate decision-making even in the face of distractions and uncertainty.'[91]

Third, shared leadership helps to de-silo the organisation. As a result, the cost of politicking drops in terms of money, time, and collateral damage caused by submerged conflicts.

Finally, shared leadership thrives on openness and trust, so that real information becomes available in real time, enhancing the quality of feedback processes.

Your choice: sharing leadership, or running with the power mongers?

Does the thought of sharing leadership frighten you? Do you feel more at home among the power mongers in your team? If so, an agile environment is probably not for you. Sadly, you'll miss out on the opportunities co-creation can offer your organisation, and you personally.

Why continue to bear the burden of making the 'right' decisions all the time when decision making and accountability can be shared?

Shared leadership might face tough resistance for another reason: many people *do* prefer a leader to tell them exactly what they need to do. Being asked to share leadership might cause resentment and leave them feeling uncertain.[92]

Then again, just as you cannot solve the problems of tomorrow with yesterday's toolkit, you cannot really soar with yesterday's approaches. Shared leadership demands that all co-workers subordinate their ego, whether that be the inflated ego or the fearful one.

Everyone should learn to enjoy the success of the collective and personally forego any credit if the group is successful.[93]

Implementing a shared leadership approach

Adopting a shared leadership model first of all implies creating space for co-creation. As we indicate earlier in this book, creating space for co-creation involves developing a great passionate vision, forming loosely coupled teams, developing *clear* but limited agile decision-making principles and establishing a challenging growth culture.

Shared leadership also involves the ability to capture and leverage the diversity of competences, views and insights within the team so that co-creation becomes a reality. There are five elements to this.

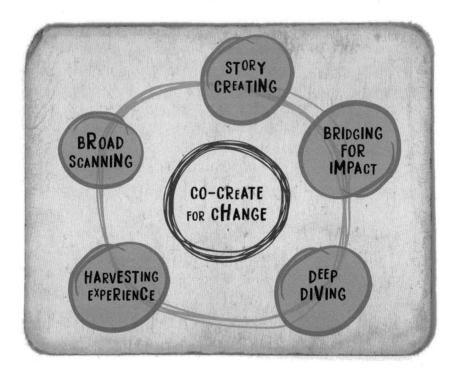

Story creating:

Story creators have the unique ability to connect smart data, future-oriented new ideas, profound experience, disruptive technologies and even vague first ideas, with great imagination and foresight into a new and strong business story. They make vague ideas tangible, as well as plot a new path and align it with the organisation's passionate vision.

Imagine yourself as being an orchestra conductor who helps team members bring forth unique sounds from their individual instruments to create a beautiful harmony. See the different and unique views expressed by your people with your leadership as a great new composition, as a 'beautiful noise'.

Your role, therefore, is to facilitate the conversations in a way that allows these different views, beliefs and ideas to be expressed constructively. The role of the story teller is to connect and energise the other team members so they can tap into and thrive on their strengths, while the story teller meanders through the richness of their ideas to find the golden thread.

Deep diving:

Just as you can no longer do without smart data systems to support your decision making; neither can you do without your top specialists and experts – your 'deep divers'. These people are the masters of advanced insights and methods in their field. While their expertise is crucial to success, they should also understand that chasing and waiting for the perfect answer slows down the quest for innovative ideas.

Sometimes good enough is perfection.

Be aware that some important decision-making biases are associated with expertise. There is the danger that they continue to use their fixed mindsets and paradigms to try and address new challenges that in reality require a different approach. Kahneman refers to this as 'what-we-see-is-all-there-is'. The more expertise we have, the greater the danger of us falling into this trap![94]

Ideally, deep divers should not be technical nerds who can't co-create with others, nor people who prefer to operate in safe silos, unencumbered by the burden of others' ideas. An agile deep diver is a person with a low need for closure, someone who can tolerate ambiguity while searching for innovative yet grounded answers.

Harvesting experience:

Digital forecasting does not always trump human forecasts. Having lived the moments of truth of your products and services helps you to understand and interpret the formal data provided by smart systems. Harvesters actively seek to find and harness the richness of implicit knowledge, which is frequently the seed for new approaches. The fact that more and more people play very temporary roles in today's organisations (e.g. they work on short-term contracts or change jobs routinely) undermines this, however, which makes nurturing the harvesting role even more important.

Broad scanning:

An innovative team can't do without adapting proactively to new technologies and trends. It must broadly scan for new information and ways of doing things. Disruptive innovation never attacks you from the front, however: it comes from the periphery. This is what 'peripheral vision' is about: an acute awareness that information and challenges may be present in places and from sources least expected. Therefore, pay close attention to changes in customer behaviour, the moves of your competitors, market disruptions, new entrants and alternative technologies. Yet be daring as well, dream the impossible, and be an adventurer in territories never explored. *Become* the one that enters a market from the periphery.

Bridging for impact:

Bridging requires an acute awareness of the potential ripple effects of new ideas developed in a soaring mode. The impact on the broader eco-context must be foreseen and evaluated. Bear in mind also that, sooner or later, a concrete mode of implementation will also be needed (rooting). This is the tricky part of the bridging role: the (valid) concern about implementation should nonetheless not hinder the creative process.

Co-create for real change

Is there a connection between the way we frame 'shared leadership' and the way we deal with change management? Of course there is.

One of the very popular, older change models is Kurt Lewin's *unfreeze – change – freeze* model, a model that perfectly fits the rooting logic: first get rid of the old operational logic, then install a new logic and 'freeze' it.[95] In a VUCA world, installing fixed, slow, controllable patterns is not a winning move. The diagram below illustrates what change within an agile organisation should be about.

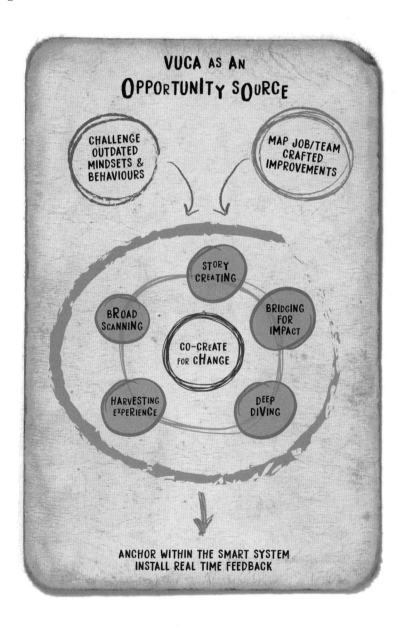

Given that organisations consist of both formal and informal systems (see part 2), change processes should start with mapping the outdated mindsets and behaviours of the formal organisation (what we referred to as 'learned helplessness'), as well as map (and so value) the small and large adaptations that are made within the informal system by individuals and teams (crafted improvements).

Both realities are a wonderful start for the next phase – co-creation for change – and to tackle the opportunity at hand. The diverse roles described above, will create paths that go beyond the existing thinking and doing.

In a third phase, the new approaches should be anchored within the organisation's smart system to enrich the decision-making capacity within all layers of the organisation. This effort includes installing a dynamic feedback process to make sure there is no 'freezing' of the new ideas. Real time feedback will ensure the system gets adapted directly. Be sure also to change your reward mechanisms accordingly, so these contribute to fast unlearning of the old way of behaving.

Just remember

More than ever before, great performance in organisations comes from great team work and great collaborative processes. Talent development, organisational structures and smart systems are important, but secondary.[96] Compose your soaring teams with people who collectively have the above competencies – story creating, deep diving, harvesting experience, broad scanning, bridging for impact – and you will be well on your way to great performance in a VUCA world. Are you ready?

Challenge
your thinking !

Question 1

* How many decisions do you take
  that your co-workers are able to take themselves?

* Is this because you don't trust them?

* If so, what needs to change – and on whose side – to
  establish trust?

Question 2

* Do you value competitive behaviours more than
  reflection and collaboration when you appoint a
  leader?

* Time for a 180° shift?

Question 3

* Do you as a leader create a space where a
  passionate vision guides people to interact in ways
  that tap into, and leverage, their strengths to create
  sustainable outcomes?

Make your choice, stay where you are OR TAKE THE LEAP!

A job within a tightly structured organisation,
where functional departments are
constantly at odds with another,
questioning the others' approaches
and motives,
while you keep knowledge carefully hidden
for your own benefit.

OR

A job within a loosely coupled organisation,
where teams collaborate across
functional and hierarchical divides,
and where you have the opportunity
and discipline
to do whatever is required
to have a sustainable impact.

Talent
on the
MOVE

The key to success is
not to do more work faster.
The key is to generate
more value from less work and
deliver it sooner.[97]

In need of a complete makeover

The role of human resources management is changing fundamentally. As
the authors of Deloitte's 2017 report, 'Rewriting the Rules for the Digital
Age', put it: 'High-performing organisations operate as empowered net-

works, coordinated through culture, information systems, and talent mobility. (...) As networks and ecosystems replace organisational hierarchies, the traditional question "For whom do you work?" has been replaced by "With whom do you work?"'[98]

Do you still have an HR toolkit that is built around lifelong employment, though most of your co-workers stay for five years, or even shorter? Do you still have reporting systems that capture the hours and minutes people work each day? Even Rip Van Winkle was more in tune with change than that!

It is time to say goodbye to the logic and tools developed in, and for, an era of hierarchical organisations for whom stability and predictability were the key criteria. The role of HR is no longer about setting up systems to manage individual performance, but about coaching for improved team performance.

Lifelong employment is a thing of the past. Talent mobility (internally and externally) is the new core assumption. Within agile organisations, HR should bring competencies together in a nimble way: assigning and re-assigning people to projects on the go. Moehrle seconds this: 'Rather than jobs and roles, work will be thought of in terms of assignments, with teams assembled from the most suitable and engaged talent to execute them.'[99]

On top of that, thanks to artificial intelligence, smart robots will take over even more rooting jobs than before, and even a lot of knowledge jobs. Here's an example: the jobs of radiologists in hospitals are at stake. In the near future, patients will be scanned by smart scanners in specialised institutions. Artificial intelligence will make the diagnosis and automatically forward the result to the medical expert. Only in exceptional cases will the intervention of a radiologist be required.[100]

While smart systems will take over many routine activities, we support this assertion by Hess: 'Human beings will still be needed to do the jobs that require higher-order critical, creative, and innovative thinking and the jobs that require high emotional engagement to meet the needs of other human beings. (...) We are confirmation-seeking thinkers and ego-affirmation-seeking defensive reasoners. We will need to overcome those proclivities in order to take our thinking, listening, relating, and collaborating skills to a much higher level. (...) The new smart will be determined not by what or how you know, but by the quality of your thinking, listening, relating, collaborating, and learning.'[101]

Those responsible for HR will find themselves at a crossroads, with their role changing from slotting individuals into jobs established according to (now outdated) HR systems to instead unleashing people's entrepreneurial potential within agile contexts. This fundamental shift in HR management will inevitably lead to some turmoil in the organisation's relationships with its employees and social partners.

WHO DO YOU NOTICE?

Katzenbach and Kahn emphasise that the formal way of describing job content aims for homogeneity, whereas the informal way of letting roles ebb and flow depending on current needs encourages individuality and innovative behaviour. Realise that opting for an 'ebb and flow' (agile) approach can cause tensions: the traditional HR approach tends to reward employees who excel at meeting the formal![102] Your reward systems should be adapted to appropriately cater for both approaches.

Five tough questions to ask, five assumptions to let go of

1. WHAT WILL REMAIN OF THE GOOD OLD FAIRNESS PRINCIPLE?

For decades social partners have been guided by the principle of fairness; e.g. what is fair compensation for doing a particular job and how does one ensure equal treatment of people doing the same or similar jobs? Thanks to this concern, most employees in the developed world are undoubtedly better off than those of 100 years ago.

But what is fairness in a world where the work environment is changing continuously and diversity is celebrated? We have moved from *job descriptions* to *task descriptions*, and from there to *describing broad roles*. In agile companies, even roles are becoming irrelevant and are replaced by a focus on competencies to be mobilised in focused, and often very short-term, projects. Even the competencies required within the project can change instantly.

Requiring that everyone be treated the same way for doing the same job makes little sense in an agile environment. Jobs, tasks and roles cannot be compared anymore in accordance with a standardised system. For a long time, for example, we used length of service and position in the company hierarchy as objective criteria for determining remuneration and benefits. Is this still relevant today? We don't think so.

Yet what does a system that rewards entrepreneurism and even celebrates failure in pursuit of innovation look like? We believe that the starting point is to look at co-workers as individuals with specific competencies and not as people belonging to particular categories (for example, white and blue collar) or having certain scholarly degrees or particular job grades.

STOP
Stop seeing jobs as a coherent cluster
of standardised tasks
that remain stable over a long period of time and
which are associated with specific payment categories.

RE-INVENT
We need to re-invent what we recruit for (competencies
versus jobs, tasks or roles),
as well as how we assess performance,
remunerate, and incentivise and promote.

② TODAY'S TALENT, TOMORROW'S 'SOCIAL PASSIVES'?

Today's agile work environment is about continuously finding new competencies and creating the space to co-create. The big advantage of continuously bringing in new talent, or re-configuring teams, is the so-called 'virgin eyes' phenomenon. Virgin eyes belong to people who are not completely embedded in the old way of thinking and doing; they bring a fresh perspective.

What does one do, however, about people whose competences are no longer needed; i.e. those who have become 'social passives'. Is it fair to let those go who served you so well before?

Replacing your computer hardware or reprogramming its software is a straightforward task – it's rather unlikely that the machine will object or demand compassion. The same is probably not true for the person whose competence you needed 12 months ago, who now finds out that his competence has become obsolete? How will this great creative brain react when you suddenly 'unplug' it?

Instead of just letting talents go, you could structure your teams and your employment relationships in a way that allows for easy redeployment of competences. Can talents who are no longer needed in a soaring context be redeployed to rooted functions, or vice versa? Can you allow people to take time off between assignments to reload their batteries and maybe even learn new skills? Do flexi-jobs offer a better structure?

Instead of providing people with lifelong employment, can you be one stop along their journey of lifelong learning?

Another important question is this: while fresh blood might be a good thing, how will you prevent losing critical implicit knowledge if you continuously replace talent? We already alluded to the importance of tapping your organisation's 'implicit' knowledge. Here we refer not merely to people's years of experience, but also the knowledge they build up both by doing and by failing. It is the latter that provides individuals and organisations with valuable experience needed to make the formal systems work.

How will you store or retain implicit knowledge if your talent is always on the move?

IMPLICIT KNOWLEDGE VERSUS FRESH TALENT

ExxonMobil took an interesting approach to balancing the need for fresh talent and retaining implicit knowledge. They have provided for 'doctor' and 'play' days when implementing their fully integrated data system. During 'doctor' days, they invite experienced rooters to play with the smart system and find bugs in it to improve the overall system. During 'play' days, they train people to get the most out of the system to simulate real-life problems, coaching the participants to find answers using the new smart system.

Luckily, at least for the immediate future, the new generation of job seekers is characterised not by a need for long-term job security, but by a desire for entrepreneurship, a hope for continuous new job opportunities, a growing need for self-development and the view that working for themselves is the most desirable career path.[103]

STOP

Stop treating individuals as if they will stay with you forever.
Lifelong employment is a thing of the past.

RE-INVENT

Competence mobility is the new core assumption.
Re-invent your HR systems to configure and re-configure teams by bringing together the right competences, at the right time and for the right purpose.

③ WHAT IMPACT WILL THE 'COMPETENCE MARKETPLACE' HAVE ON RECRUITMENT?

The time when we recruited on the basis of formal qualifications, years of experience, and so on, is almost over. Today's recruitment is about finding the right competences for the moment and ensuring that new talents can quickly become empowered. This goes beyond merely finding the right set of technical competences. What you need are individuals who are also entrepreneurial, able to co-create with others and confident enough to risk failure in pursuit of innovation. Don't neglect the critical importance of the right attitude (an agile mindset) either, as well as a strong commitment to your passionate vision.

Moehrle pleads for an approach whereby organisations create 'talent marketplaces' – we prefer the term 'competence' marketplace.[104] These 'virtual' markets match competencies (knowledge, skills, etc.) with work assignments. This offers people more opportunities to excel, because it enables talent 'to leverage the full spectrum of business assignments to grow and navigate their career, matching personal preferences with work opportunities – and sustaining their own employability.' From a 'war' for talent, organisations evolve towards a 'war' for competencies!

The competence marketplace takes over. And if this is the case, should we tax artificial intelligence of robots, providing income for our social security systems?

STOP
Stop recruiting on the basis of formal qualifications and demographic characteristics. Don't merely reward people for position.

RE-INVENT
Search for competencies.

④ 'ALL NOSES SHOULD POINT IN THE SAME DIRECTION' ... CERTAINLY NOT!

In Dutch, there is a saying that 'all noses should point in the same direction'. It is a mantra familiar to many rooted organisations and is handy for guarding fiefdoms and holding on to power. Most experiments with self-organising teams fail because the organisational context with its top-down control system and 'moving in the same direction' philosophy does not allow the kind of freedom needed to promote true innovation. Traditional leaders want sameness to be able to remain in control.

Sameness kills creativity and innovation. It is diversity that stimulates innovation.

To reinvent your organisation, you need a diversity of ideas and competencies. Agile environments operate on a 'power unplugged' basis and encourage operating at multiple speeds. Modular and optimally diverse teams form and later recombine according to the needs of the moment.[105] Agile leaders need to be comfortable with 'multiple-speed' solutions.

Your new mantra? Amateurs compete, professionals (co-)create. Make this maxim obligatory.

STOP
Stop demanding that
'all noses should point in the same direction'.

RE-INVENT
Can you see diversity of ideas, approaches,
techniques and mindsets
as catalysts for innovation?
Allow for agile 'speedboats' moving in different
directions from the slow and cumbersome mother ship
to search for new ideas and inventions,
free from the constraints of uniformity and hierarchy!

Diversity is not only about differences in demographic characteristics. If, for example, a team of five women and five men have the same cognitive style, you end up with a homogeneous, non-diverse team.

⑤ DIGITISATION: THE LUBRICANT OF THE COMING DECADES?

Digitisation plays a major role in setting up smart systems that can aid and sustain decision making in both soaring and in rooting environments. These systems not only provide integrated data (which is crucial for grasping and understanding ripple effects), but sometimes also take over the decision making itself.

From a talent management perspective, part of that integrated data system should allow you to map competencies so that, for example, you can compose and re-compose project teams on a continuous basis, track their progress, and assess the quality and impact of their decision making.

Following the example of top sports coaches – and with the permission of your co-workers, of course – you might even want to consider monitoring on their health on a 24-hour basis. Apps are already available, for example, to detect overly high levels of stress or early signs of burnout. Couldn't this dramatically improve those static, boring, unproductive and sometimes downright dishonest performance reviews?

Paraphrasing Aghina, De Smet and Weerda, we believe that in agile environments performance management should involve a move away from a top-down target-setting and periodic static assessment to a set of performance metrics jointly owned across the innovative value chain and provided by an integrated monitoring system.[106]

STOP
Stop worrying about Big Brother watching you.

RE-INVENT
Ask yourself how integrated data can help you
improve things like team composition
and decision making.
Gather information, monitor performance and
reward not only success
but also 'entrepreneurial' failure.

So, do we just ignore the human element?

As we have said, organisations are not in need of particular individuals, they need specific competencies. For many, this will create uncertainty about longer-term job security and advancement. This is an obvious, and hard reality.

But consider this: within traditional organisations we compartmentalise people in silos and fence them in. Once a year, they are evaluated on their output in line with their prescribed tasks and objectives. The more they live up to the standardised criteria, the higher their chances for reward and promotion. Their true, creative talent is hidden away behind these regulated processes. In highly bureaucratic organisations, great, well-paid talent is straitjacketed by hierarchical power. This is another hard reality.

We have no choice but to leave the old ways of managing people behind. We need to put selecting for and managing competences at the forefront. We need a new toolkit so that HR can connect again to its eco-context, one where employees are given the freedom to succeed.

'Work will be liberated from the alienated
form it took on in the industrial age.
The rise of a new breed of professionals
will have much more in common with Renaissance
master artisans than the blue- or white-collar
workers we are used to:
proud of what they do and what they create,
working with passion and purpose,
and nurturing their personal reputation and brand.'
Tomas Chamorro-Premuzic[107]

Is this description overly optimistic? Probably, but do try to envisage how your role as a people manager could shift to be aligned with the demands of agility. And if your field is HR management, shouldn't you, together with your social partners, start thinking of building that new toolkit for an agile reality?

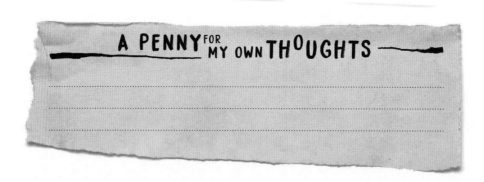

A PENNY FOR MY OWN THOUGHTS

Question 1

✳ *Can you live with the idea that working conditions for soarers and for rooters can be very different?*

Question 2

✳ *Why do organisations in a VUCA world stick with static measurement systems built to measure repeatable and stable things?*

✳ *How dynamic, for example, are your staff evaluation and reward systems?*

Question 3

✳ *How will you adapt your recruitment system to the new reality?*

✳ *How will you contribute to the talent marketplace?*

✳ *How will you fairly deal with competences when you no longer need them?*

✳ *How will our society set up its educational systems (schools and life-long learning) to make sure that new competencies can be acquired quickly?*

Make your choice, stay where you are OR TAKE THE LEAP!

My organisation has all the formal
quality labels in its sector.
Many internal assessment
tools indicate how we enhanced our
performance over
the past years.

OR

Our approach is that feedback systems
should open the doors for innovation,
instead of making people cling
to the status quo.
Instead of slavishly following what
worked for us or others until now,
we continuously invest in reinventing
ourselves.

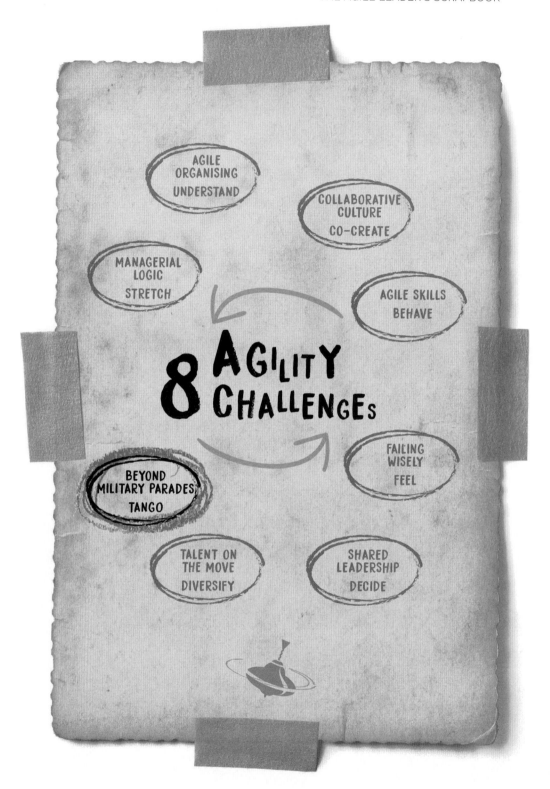

AGILITY CHALLENGE 8

From **MILITARY PARADES** to dancing **the tango**

> '**I**f you feel like everything is under
> control,
> you don't go fast enough.'
> —Mario Andretti

Becoming agile poses particular challenges for large, established organisations. Typically, they are oriented toward managing scale applying the logic of standardised quality. While the biggest players out there have built their fame and fortunes on a rooting strategy, they are often fragile in the face of turbulence, lacking the flexibility to learn and adapt fast. Hamel sees several reasons for this.[108]

One obvious reason is that by becoming bigger and bigger, the risk of collapsing under the weight of their own complexity becomes very real. Further, a lot of decisions are made 'on an Olympian peak', which means that the decision-making process and its outcomes are decoupled from what is really happening; i.e. on the work floor or customer interface. More approval layers also slow down the time it takes to react to changes in the environment.

Hamel's third vulnerability: in a hierarchy, the power to overturn, kill or modify another's new idea is often vested in a single person. That person's parochial interests may not only skew decisions, but also systematically disempower lower level employees. In any event, chances are that new initiatives are subjected to so many review layers and controls to ensure that mistakes aren't made or repeated, which means the benefits of entrepreneurship and agility are eroded, often completely.[109]

Can big, hierarchical organisations that apply only a rooted philosophy ever become agile as well? Here's some food for thought.

Don't collapse under the weight of complexity: abandon the illusion that creating one big, uniform organisation will save costs

Have you ever seen a case where obliging subsidiary organisations to strictly apply the same rules and procedures as the mother organisation strengthened the former's performance? Indeed, they may have become easier to control and to compare, but this setting of blanket rules likely killed their entrepreneurial potential, the very reason you acquired them in the first place.

Being governed by identical rules, making every unit follow the same operational logic, is great when it comes to military parades. Within an organisational context, chances are high that this enforced logic completely disregards the diversity of the unique ecosystem of each unit. This causes many acquisitions to underperform, even fail. The illusion that sameness is better, serves only to dominate others and creates the illusion of being in control. Governing your organisation in a VUCA environment requires that your board members understand both the rooting and the soaring logic; otherwise they will stay in their one-sided rooting logic and harm the board's decision-making capacity.

Conquer the Olympian peak: create a space for rooting and soaring to coexist

By definition, big organisations will always need to root part of their activities. But it is evident that, in a VUCA world, no organisation can do without massive soaring capacity, where co-workers and units are rewarded for innovation and disruptive activities. To make sure these two worlds can coexist, even leverage off each other, organisations should develop a mindset that allows for fostering the strengths of both.

Start by providing complete transparency about which mode you are in; i.e. soaring or rooting. As discussed earlier, these two realities shouldn't be in competition with each other, but be complementary. Knowing which dance your partner wants to dance is of great help when you are on the dance floor! There is a critical point at which rooting is not the answer, and soaring is. There is also a time to stop soaring and hand over the reins to strong rooters.

You should ban data systems that only cater for the information needs of particular units or silos and instead invest in integrated smart data systems in which the ripple effects across silos are at the centre of the information provided. What is even more important is to give every co-worker access to the data they need for enhanced and quick decision making.

Fast, transparent knowledge-sharing is crucial. There should be no artificial firewalls, installed merely to enhance your own power.

The workplace should be conducive to co-creation (see part 3). This includes the physical space too. Most workplaces are designed for enhancing rooting. We suggest that you consider creating separate physical spaces for soaring, where people can, in a fairly unencumbered way, explore, experiment and discover new horizons. Do your meeting spaces allow for this?

Conquering the Olympian peak will not be possible unless co-workers can identify and address the uncertainties that come with the growth mindset (see part 5). Leaders and managers should unlearn their traditional, repetitive dance moves that allowed them to evaluate organisational and individual performance in terms of what worked in the past. To build for the future, managers should be eager to learn new ways of doing things and embrace agile thinking methods.

Don't be dependent on power mongering while innovating: hire a sniper to get rid of your 'murder' boards

Murder boards are all organisational committees that slow down or even kill innovative initiatives. Relying on them to assess such initiatives is a bad practice. Picture them in your mind's eye: specially appointed committees to 'guard' new initiatives. They apply the existing rules, procedures, budgetary constraints and rooting mindset to assess a new idea. Predictably, the outcome will be more of the same; new initiatives will be made to fit into the old logic, or they will not receive the green light at all. Radical ideas focused on a disruptive future will be rejected as naive or insurgent.

Most probably,
those who
staff your murder
boards don't understand
the art of soaring.

It is a good idea to reinvent the way you evaluate new opportunities. Don't start with the traditional business plan – it's far too slow and we know that going for perfection hinders innovation. In a rooting environment, ideas for improvement are tied to a business plan. In a soaring environment, new ideas are explored through clever experimentation.

Experimentation is the new game. Whether large or small, your organisation should create some 'useful slack' to allow agile project teams to play around with certain ideas and plans before firming them up into a definite plan. Instead of starting with the plan and developing ideas based on that, you start with the ideas and build possibilities around those, only then looking for more concrete evidence that the idea could work.[110] Sure, this takes extra time. We've said it before though: sometimes you have to go slow to move fast!

Investing in perfection
will only waste time and resources;
rather apply the 'is-it-good-enough-
to-experiment-with?' principle.

Refrain from using today's best practices as a starting point, as they limit your creativity. The question of how to create sustainable value aligned with the passionate vision of the company, should guide your thinking.

Replace murder boards by small groups of visionary people from inside and outside the organisation who are not afraid to dream and able to skilfully improvise, just how the tango is danced. Their main aim should be to encourage idea generation and experimentation before selecting the most promising ones for implementation.

A PENNY FOR MY OWN THOUGHTS

Time to tango[111]

'**S**ometimes in life confusion tends to arise and only dialogue of dance seems to make sense.'
—Shah Asad Rizvi

For organisations to become agile, a change in corporate culture, vision and values is needed. This implies a shift in mindset away from one focused on competing to survive or beat the competition, to one that favours collaborating for sustainable impact; a shift from silo mentalities to openness; a shift from making decisions in elite circles to allowing co-workers a meaningful 'voice' in decision making. Leaders should discourage behaviours that destroy trust or prevent innovative development, and instead reward behaviours that promote co-creation, innovation and entrepreneurship.

One vehicle for achieving this is *organisational improvisation*; that is, the combination of planning and implementing that happens on the spot.[112] While the term 'improvisation' is mostly used in an artistic environment, organisations increasingly use 'improv' techniques to react quickly and intuitively to address problems that suddenly emerge.[113] Many of the divergent thinking skills we mentioned earlier in this book, support improvisation.

IF YOU TOOK A PICTURE OF YOUR ORGANISATION, WHAT WOULD IT LOOK LIKE: A MILITARY PARADE OR THE TANGO ?

As we stated in the beginning of this book, we wanted you to rethink the underlying logic of the organisational principles you and your organisation hold dear at the moment. In the process, we have identified *eight key agility challenges* to master, if you want to become more agile. Admittedly none of them is straightforward, but don't panic. As Quinn said: 'When we commit to a vision to do something that has never been done before, there is no way to know how to get there. We simply have to build the bridge as we walk on it.'[114] So, when embarking on an agile journey, keep your eye on your longer term vision, experiment and innovate as you move towards it, yet also be prepared to fail 'wisely' along the way.

WHEN SOARING

Stay connected with your dream

Feel at ease stepping off the
well-trodden paths

Take the minority of one seriously:
uniqueness is the new fair

Aggressively pursue co-creation

Experiment, fail wisely, learn fast

Allow and encourage people to question
the way things are done

Be the master of the ripple effect

Plan for fast adaptation, don't dwell
on the possible risks

Create your own best practices

	ROOTING	SOARING
The biggest plus	Standardised quality	Innovative moves
Building blocks	Clear-cut activities, formally described and controlled	Autonomous, flexible teams and initiatives, loosely coupled
Mindset	Build to last, strive for perfection, uniformity is key	Flexibility, support for failing wisely, embracing diversity
Focus	Strengthening the rings of the chain is the path to total quality	Holism: the whole is greater than the sum of its parts
People	Clarifying who is responsible and accountable for what	Bringing in needed competences, facilitating co-creation
Change	Top-down and continuous improvement based on smart data	Self-induced change through experimentation supported by smart data
The big schism	Only actions from the formal organisation are acknowledged	Support for unofficial agreed-upon processes to create nimbleness
Outside	Conform to the institutional environment	Fast and flexible reactions to changes in the eco-context
Foundation	Specialised boxed knowledge	Collective intelligence
Aim	To be the best in the existing cohort	Innovate and create a sustainable ripple effect
Crippled	Cannot exhaustively predict the dynamics of a VUCA context	Positional corporate culture and lack of co-creation abilities among co-workers
False	Hoping to change the world without expecting the reverse to happen	Individualistic behaviour will be compensated for by serving the whole
Biggest challenge	Building one big smart system, making decisional impact clear	Getting rid of the traditional managerial control freak mindset
Advice	'Not seeing a tsunami or an economic event coming is excusable; building something fragile to them is not' - N.N. Taleb	Assess the tsunami of possibilities; filter out the noise.
Control	The leader is in control	Distributed among the members of the group

Notes & extra reading

1   Toffler, A. (1970). *Future shock*. New York: Random House. Toffler, A. & Toffler, H. (1984). *The adaptive corporation*. New York: McGraw-Hill.

2   In the back of our minds we wonder why the corporate world seems to have learnt nothing over the years from dancing elephants or the concept of the learning organisation. Collins, J. (2001). *Good to great: why some companies make the leap... and others don't*. New York: HarperCollins. Belasco, J.A. (1991). *Teaching the elephant to dance: the manager's guide to empowering change*. New York: Penguin Books. Senge, P. (1990). *The fifth discipline. The art and practice of the learning organization*. New York: Doubleday Business.

3   Heifetz, R.A. & Laurie, D.L. (1997). Leaders do not need to know all the answers. They do need to ask the right questions. Reprinted by permission from *Harvard Business Review*, January-February issue. http://www4.ncsu.edu/unity/users/p/padilla/www/435-Leadership/Heifetz%20and%20Laurie%20The%20work%20of%20leadership.pdf (last accessed September 2017).

4   Hannula, E. (2016). The economy of speed – better late or inaccurate? http://qualityintelligence.net/articles/the-economy-of-speed-better-late-or-inaccurate (last accessed January 2017).

5   Reeves, M. & Deimler, M. (2011). Adaptability: the new competitive advantage. *Harvard Business Review*, July-August issue. https://hbr.org/2011/07/adaptability-the-new-competitive-advantage (last accessed February 2017).

6   Paju, S. (2015). Adaptiveness is the new efficiency. https://www.linkedin.com/pulse/adaptiveness-new-efficiency-sami-paju (last accessed February 2017).

7   Aghina, W., De Smet, A. & Weerda, K. (2015). Agility: it rhymes with stability. *McKinsey Quarterly*, December. http://www.mckinsey.com/business-functions/organization/our-insights/agility-it-rhymes-with-stability (last accessed April 2017).

8   Paju, S. (2015). Adaptiveness is the new efficiency. https://www.linkedin.com/pulse/adaptiveness-new-efficiency-sami-paju (last accessed February 2017).

9   Others refer to this as 'dynamic stability': Teece, D.G., Pisano, J. & Shuen, A. (1997). Dynamic capabilities and strategic management. *Strategic Management Journal*. Volume 18(7).

10 Paju, S. (2015). Adaptiveness is the new efficiency. https://www.linkedin.com/pulse/adaptiveness-new-efficiency-sami-paju (last accessed February 2017).

11 Von Schantz, J. (2016). Agility is about discipline. http://qualityintelligence.net/articles/agility-is-about-discipline (last accessed February 2017).

12 https://en.wikipedia.org/wiki/Buzzword_bingo (last accessed December 2016).

13 We highly recommend this article on the difference between a philosophy that focuses on creating shareholder value and one focused on a broader objective: Bower, J.L. & Paine L.S. (2017). The error at the heart of corporate leadership. *Harvard Business Review*, May-June issue. https://hbr.org/2017/05/managing-for-the-long-term (last accessed 19 June 2017).

14 Old Zen story, author unknown.

15 As a warm up: chaos is an order not yet discovered: https://www.youtube.com/watch?v=G2xFJUSLEv8 (last accessed August 2017) or https://www.youtube.com/watch?v=Hp8wGQW-Y48 (last accessed July 2017).

16   http://webecoist.momtastic.
com/2008/09/07/17-amazing-examples-of-
fractals-in-nature/ (last accessed March
2017).

17   'A fractal is a mathematical set that
exhibits a repeating pattern displayed
at every scale'. https://en.wikipedia.
org/wiki/Fractal (last accessed February 2017). The source Wikipedia uses
is: Boeing, G. (2016). Visual analysis of
nonlinear dynamical systems: chaos,
fractals, self-similarity and the limits
of prediction. *Systems*, Volume 4(4). If
you are interested in more please start
by surfing: http://fractalfoundation.org/
fractivities/WhatIsaFractal-1pager.pdf
and http://fractalfoundation.org/fractiv-
ities/FractalPacks-EducatorsGuide.pdf
(both last accessed February 2017).

18   https://www.youtube.com/
watch?v=V-mCuFYfJdI (last accessed
February 2017). And https://www.you-
tube.com/watch?v=OlmDVuxerQ0 (last
accessed February 2017).

19   For some, 'loosely coupled' might
be a relatively new concept, but for
specialists in the field of organisational
behaviour it is a classic concept http://
dimetic.dime-eu.org/dimetic_files/
OrtonWeickAMR1990.pdf (last accessed
February 2017). Orton, J.D. & Weick,
K.E. (1990). Loosely coupled systems:
a reconceptualization. *The Academy of
Management Review*, Volume 15(2).

20   Reeves, M. & Deimler, M. (2011). Adaptability: the new competitive advantage.
Harvard Business Review, July-August
issue. https://hbr.org/2011/07/adaptabil-
ity-the-new-competitive-advantage (last
accessed February 2017).

21   https://en.wikipedia.org/wiki/Attractor
(last accessed March 2017).

22   Actual origin uncertain but probably
from Antoine de Saint-Exupéry, http://
quoteinvestigator.com/2015/08/25/sea/
(last accessed January 2017).

23   Kenney, S. (2010). Creating adaptive
organizations. American Management
Association. http://www.amanet.org/
training/articles/creating-adaptive-or-
ganizations.aspx (last accessed August
2017).

24   Nordström, K.A. & Ridderstråle, J. (2002).
Funky business: talent makes capital dance.
London: Pearson Education Ltd.

25   Holbeche, L. (2017). *The Agile Organization. How to build an innovative, sustainable
and resilient business.* London: KoganPage.

26   Klein, G. (2007). Performing a project
premortem. *Harvard Business Review*, September issue. https://hbr.org/2007/09/
performing-a-project-premortem (last
accessed February 2017). A premortem is the hypothetical opposite of a
postmortem. A premortem in a business
setting comes at the beginning of a
project rather than at the end, so that
the project can be improved rather
than dissected after the fact. Unlike
a typical critiquing session, in which
team members are asked what might go
wrong, the premortem operates on the
assumption that the 'patient' has in fact
died, and so asks what did go wrong.
The team members' task is to generate
plausible reasons for the project's failure.

27   Old Zen story, author unknown.

28   https://en.wikipedia.org/wiki/Co-crea-
tion (last accessed July 2017).

29   McKee, D., Varadarajan, R. & Pride,
W.M. (1989). Strategic adaptability and
firm performance: a market-contingent
perspective. *Journal of Marketing*, Volume
53(3).

30   Oktemgil, M. & Greenley, G. (1997).
Consequences of high and low
adaptive capability in UK companies.
European Journal of Marketing, Volume
31(7). *http://www.emeraldinsight.com/
doi/full/10.1108/03090569710176619* (last
accessed February 2017).

31   Old Zen story, author unknown.

32 Kay, J.A. (2010). *Obliquity: why our goals are best achieved indirectly*. New York: Penguin Books. John Kay clearly indicates that the linear approach is not the fastest one. He gives an abundance of examples why we should accept and honour the fact that most managerial practices are characterised as 'muddling or meandering through'.

33 https://www.nps.gov/fire/wildland-fire/what-we-do/wildfires-prescribed-fires-and-fuels.cfm (last accessed February 2017).

34 http://www.ignitedquotes.com/trusting-you-is-my-decision-proving-me-right-is-your-choice/ (last accessed March 2017).

35 Hardin, R. (2002). *Trust and trustworthiness*. New York: Russel Sage Foundation.

36 Taleb, N.N. (2012). *Antifragile: things that gain from disorder*. New York: Random House.

37 Heiligtag, S. & Webb, A. (2017). A case study in combating bias. *McKinsey Quarterly*. http://www.mckinsey.com/business-functions/organization/our-insights/a-case-study-in-combating-bias (last accessed May 2017).

38 McDermott, I & Hal, C.M. (2016). *The collaborative leader*. London: Crown House Publishing.

39 Nicholson, N. (2000). *Managing the human animal*. London: Texere Publishing.

40 Quick, M.S. & Feldman, M.S. (2011). Distinguishing participation and inclusion. *Journal of Planning Education and Research*. Volume 31(3).

41 Verwaeren, B. (2017). *It ain't what you do, it's the way that you do it. The effect of accountability focus on individual exploratory search*. Dissertation submitted at Ghent University, Faculty of Economics and Business Administration.

42 Denning, S. (2016). Garry Hamel: can big firms be agile? *Forbes*, November issue. https://www.forbes.com/sites/stevedenning/2016/11/27/gary-hamel-can-big-firms-be-agile/#1f81f37138c5 (last accessed February 2017).

43 Katsikopoulos K.V & King A.J. (2010). Swarm intelligence in animal groups: when can a collective out-perform an expert? http://journals.plos.org/plosone/article?id=10.1371/journal.pone.0015505 (last accessed February 2017).

44 Bonchek refers to principles such as these 'installing the decision-making doctrine': Bonchek, M. (2016). How leaders can let go without losing control. *Harvard Business Review*, June issue. https://hbr.org/2016/06/how-leaders-can-let-go-without-losing-control (last accessed February 2017).

45 Reeves, M. & Deimler, M. (2011). Adaptability: the new competitive advantage. *Harvard Business Review*, July-August issue. https://hbr.org/2011/07/adaptability-the-new-competitive-advantage (last accessed May 2017).

46 Atkinson, J. & Moffat, S.R. (2005). *The agile organisation. From informal networks to complex effects and agility*. CCRP-publication series. (credit to the DoD Command and Control Research Program, Washington, D.C.). http://www.dodccrp.org/files/Atkinson_Agile.pdf (last accessed December 2016).

47 Wetzel, R. & Van Driel, R. (2014). The three faces of organisations as embedding for improvisation. Paper presented at World Congress of Applied Improvisation, Texas, United States. Kühl, S. (2015): *Organisations. A systems approach*. London: Routledge.

48 Reeves, M. & Deimler, M. (2011). Adaptability: the new competitive advantage. *Harvard Business Review*, July-August issue. https://hbr.org/2011/07/adaptability-the-new-competitive-advantage (last accessed May 2017).

49 Fisher, R., Ury, W. & Paton, B. (2011). *Getting to yes: negotiating agreement without giving in*. New York: Penguin.

50   Thompson, D.S., Butkus, G., Colquitt, A. & Boudreau, J. (2016). The right kind of conflict leads to better products. *Harvard Business Review*, December issue. https://hbr.org/2016/12/the-right-kind-of-conflict-leads-to-better-products (last accessed May 2017).

51   Harari, Y.N. (2011). *Sapiens. A brief history of humankind*. London: Vintage Books.

52   Collins, J.C. & Porras, J.I. (1994). *Built to last: successful habits of visionary companies*. New York: HarperCollins.

53   Aesop – Retold by Rohini Chowdhury. http://www.longlongtimeago.com/once-upon-a-time/fables/from-aesop/the-lion-with-bad-breath/ (last accessed September 2017).

54   Purcell, J. & Hall, M. (2012). Voice and participation in the modern workplace: challenges and prospects. ACAS Future of Workplace Relations. http://www.acas.org.uk/media/pdf/g/7/Voice_and_Participation_in_the_Modern_Workplace_challenges_and_prospects.pdf (last accessed February 2017).

55   Kim, W.C. & Mauborgne, R. (2003). Fair process: managing in the knowledge economy. *Harvard Business Review*, January issue. https://hbr.org/2003/01/fair-process-managing-in-the-knowledge-economy (last accessed April 2017).

56   Botelho, E.L, Powell, R.K., Kincaid, S. & Wang, D. (2017). What sets successful CEOs apart. *Harvard Business Review*, May-June issue. https://hbr.org/2017/05/what-sets-successful-ceos-apart (last accessed August 2017).

57   Gregersen, H. (2017). Bursting the CEO bubble. Why executives should talk less and ask more questions. *Harvard Business Review*, March-April issue. https://hbr.org/2017/03/bursting-the-ceo-bubble (last accessed July 2017).

58   Kenney, S. (2010). Creating adaptive organizations. American Management Association. http://www.amanet.org/training/articles/creating-adaptive-organizations.aspx (last accessed August 2017).

59   See http://quoteinvestigator.com/2014/03/09/as-we-are/ (last accessed June 2017).

60   Reeves, M. & Deimler, M. (2011). Adaptability: the new competitive advantage. *Harvard Business Review*, July-August issue. https://hbr.org/2011/07/adaptability-the-new-competitive-advantage (last accessed May 2017).

61   Kenney, S. (2010). Creating adaptive organizations. American Management Association. http://www.amanet.org/training/articles/creating-adaptive-organizations.aspx (last accessed August 2017).

62   From Polman, P. As quoted in Lewis, M.W., Andriopoulos, C. & Smith, W.K. (2014). Paradoxical leadership to enable strategic agility. *California Management Review*, Volume 56(3). https://pdfs.semanticscholar.org/9337/5978f720cf866de7a-2f8959212373ae50bb0.pdf (last accessed August 2017).

63   Atkinson, J. & Moffat, S.R. (2005). *The agile organisation. From informal networks to complex effects and agility*. CCRP-publication series. (credit to the DoD Command and Control Research Program, Washington, D.C.). http://www.dodccrp.org/files/Atkinson_Agile.pdf (last accessed December 2016).

64   Attributed to Denis Waitley. https://www.forbes.com/sites/ekaterinawalter/2013/12/30/30-powerful-quotes-on-failure/#29c7e95824bd (last accessed June 2017).

65   Sir Richard Branson as quoted at https://www.virgin.com/richard-branson/you-learn-doing-and-falling-over (last accessed June 2017).

66   Valcour, M. (2015). 4 ways to become a better learner. *Harvard Business Review*, December issue. https://hbr.org/2015/12/4-ways-to-become-a-better-learner (last accessed June 2017).

67   Gino, F. & Staats, B. (2015). Why organisations don't learn. *Harvard Business Review*, November issue. https://hbr.org/2015/11/why-organizations-dont-learn (last accessed March 2017).

68   Michael Jordan as quoted in Goldman, R. & Papson, S. (1998). *Nike culture: the sign of the swoosh*. London: Sage Publications.

69   Meyer, T. (2015). Leading a VUCA-fit organization. *USB-executive development*. http://www.usb-ed.com/WatchReadListen/Pages/Leading-a-VUCA-fit-organisation.aspx (last accessed May 2017).

70   Viscott, D. (1983). *Risking*. New York: Pocket Books.

71   Kenney, S. (2010). Creating adaptive organizations. American Management Association. http://www.amanet.org/training/articles/creating-adaptive-organizations.aspx (last accessed August 2017).

72   Author unknown.

73   The classic article is that of Lindblom, C. (1959). The science of 'muddling through'. *Public Administration Review*, Volume 19(2).

74   Attributed to Johann Wolfgang von Goethe.

75   Caddell, J. (S.D.). How to bounce back from a big mistake. (99U) http://99u.com/articles/7089/how-to-bounce-back-from-a-big-mistake (last accessed June 2017).

76   Nordström, K.A. & Ridderstråle, J. (2002). *Funky business: talent makes capital dance*. London: Pearson Education Ltd.

77   Valcour, M. (2015). 4 ways to become a better learner. *Harvard Business Review*, December issue. https://hbr.org/2015/12/4-ways-to-become-a-better-learner (last accessed June 2017).

78   Kahneman, D. (2011). *Thinking, fast and slow*. London: Penguin Group.

79   See http://www.history.com/topics/challenger-disaster (last accessed June 2017).

80   Heiligtag, S. & Webb, A. (2017). A case study in combating bias. *McKinsey Quarterly*. http://www.mckinsey.com/business-functions/organization/our-insights/a-case-study-in-combating-bias (last accessed May 2017).

81   The biases behind these questions are called (in order of the questions): availability bias and recency effect, easy retrievable, endowment effect, escalation of commitment, anchoring effect, confirmation bias, affect heuristic, outcome bias, social proof, hybris syndrome!

82   Attributed to Peter Drucker. http://www.azquotes.com/quote/521436 (last accessed April 2017).

83   The so-called 'VUCA Prime' developed by Johansen, B. (2012). *Leaders make the future: ten new leadership skills for an uncertain world*. San Francisco: Berret-Koehler.

84   Botelho, E.L, Powell, R.K., Kincaid, S. & Wang, D. (2017). What sets successful CEOs apart. *Harvard Business Review*, May-June issue. https://hbr.org/2017/05/what-sets-successful-ceos-apart (last accessed August 2017).

85   Randolph, P. (2010). 'Compulsory mediation?' *New Law Journal*. https://www.newlawjournal.co.uk/content/litigation-v-mediation (last accessed February 2017).

86   Diamond, J. (1997). *Why is sex fun? The evolution of human sexuality*. New York: Basic Books.

87   Harari, Y.N. (2011). *Sapiens. A brief history of humankind*. London: Vintage Books.

88   Reeves, M. & Deimler, M. (2011). Adaptability: the new competitive advantage. *Harvard Business Review*, July-August issue. https://hbr.org/2011/07/adaptability-the-new-competitive-advantage (last accessed May 2017).

89   Author unknown (see also https://www.linkedin.com/pulse/parables-leadership-the-wheel-light-sia-ekleader).

90   Kuhl, S., Schnelle, T. & Tillmann, F-J. (2005). Lateral leadership: an organizational approach to change. *Journal of Change Management*, Volume 5(2).

91 Couzin, I.D. (2009). Collective cognition in animal groups. *Trends In Cognitive Sciences*, Volume 13(1).

92 Cross, R., Rebele, R. & Grant, A. (2016). Collaborative overload. *Harvard Business Review*, February issue. https://hbr.org/2016/01/collaborative-overload (last accessed May 2017).

93 Lash, R. (2012). The collaboration imperative. *Ivey Business Journal*, January/February. http://iveybusinessjournal.com/publication/the-collaboration-imperative/ (last accessed February 2017).

94 Kahneman, D. (2011). *Thinking, fast and slow*. New York: Macmillan.

95 Lewin, K. (1947). Frontiers in group dynamics. *Human Relations*, Volume 1(5). http://lchc.ucsd.edu/MCA/Mail/xmcamail.2013_07.dir/pdfeF83xvxgaM.pdf (last accessed September 2017).

96 For some very interesting insights around the quality of decision making see: De Smet, A., Lackey, G. & Weiss, L.M. (2017). Untangling your organization's decision making. *McKinsey Quarterly*, June. http://www.mckinsey.com/business-functions/organization/our-insights/untangling-your-organizations-decision-making?cid=other-eml-alt-mkq-mck-oth-1706&hl-kid=58f8ec3b737641baa-2500ca18d10e0a7&hctky=1543207&hd-pid=1159abee-cf16-4c8c-b8a5-b38463d-1c4ee (last accessed June 2017).

97 Denning, S. (2016). What is agile? https://www.forbes.com/sites/stevedenning/2016/08/13/what-is-agile/#-13b30e3126e3 (last accessed June 2017).

98 Bersin, J., and others, (2017). *The organization of the future. Arriving now.* In: Rewriting the rules for the digital age. Deloitte Global Human Capital Trends: Deloitte University Press. https://www2.deloitte.com/content/dam/Deloitte/global/Documents/HumanCapital/hc-2017-global-human-capital-trends-gx.pdf (last accessed June 2017).

99 Moehrle, M. (2017). Towards a marketplace approach to managerial talent. In: EFMD Global Focus, *The EFMD Business Magazine*, Volume 1(11). http://globalfocusmagazine.com/wp-content/uploads/2017/02/EFMD-Global-Focus_1101_ONLINE.pdf (last accessed February 2017).

100 Interview with senior radiologist in the Belgian health care sector.

101 Hess, E. (2017). In the AI age, "being smart" will mean something completely different. *Harvard Business Review*, June issue. https://hbr.org/2017/06/in-the-ai-age-being-smart-will-mean-something-completely-different?utm_campaign=hbr&utm_source=twitter&utm_medium=social (last accessed July 2017).

102 Katzenbach, J.R. & Khan, Z. (2010). *Leading outside the lines*. San Francisco: Jossey-Bass.

103 Chamorro-Premuzic, T. (2017). *The talent delusion. The new psychology of human potential*. London: Piatkus.

104 Moehrle, M. (2017). Towards a marketplace approach to managerial talent. In: EFMD Global Focus, *The EFMD Business Magazine*, Volume 1(11). http://globalfocusmagazine.com/wp-content/uploads/2017/02/EFMD-Global-Focus_1101_ONLINE.pdf (last accessed February 2017).

105 Reeves, M. & Deimler, M. (2011). Adaptability: the new competitive advantage. *Harvard Business Review*, July-August issue. https://hbr.org/2011/07/adaptability-the-new-competitive-advantage (last accessed May 2017).

106 Aghina, W., De Smet, A. & Weerda, K. (2015). Agility: it rhymes with stability. *McKinsey Quarterly*, December. http://www.mckinsey.com/business-functions/organization/our-insights/agility-it-rhymes-with-stability (last accessed August, 2017).

107 Moehrle, M. (2017). Towards a market-place approach to managerial talent. In: EFMD Global Focus, *The EFMD Business Magazine*, Volume 1(11). http://globalfocusmagazine.com/wp-content/uploads/2017/02/EFMD-Global-Focus_1101_ONLINE.pdf (last accessed February 2017).

108 Hamel, G. (2011). First, let's fire all the managers. *Harvard Business Review*, December issue. https://hbr.org/2011/12/first-lets-fire-all-the-managers (last accessed July 2017).

109 Rigby, D.K., Sutherland, J. & Takeuchi, H. (2016). Embracing agile. *Harvard Business Review*, May issue. https://hbr.org/2016/05/embracing-agile (last accessed May 2017).

110 Holbeche, L. (2017). *The agile organization. How to build an innovative, sustainable and resilient business.* London: KoganPage.

111 In using the tango metaphor, we wish to acknowledge the inspiration we received from our colleague, professor Ralf Wetzel. Wetzel, R. & Nees, F. (2017). Asymmetry revisited. What leadership can learn from tango Argentino. *SCMS Indian Journal of Management*, Volume 14(2). See also Davis, K. (2015). *Dancing tango: passionate encounters in a globalizing world.* New York: New York University Press.

112 Moorman, C. & Miner, A.S. (1998). Organizational improvisation and organizational memory. *The Academy of Management Review*, Volume 23(4).

113 Verbrugge, T. (2016). *Adaptive organizations: the informal organization reinvented.* Master's thesis. Master of Science in Business Administration. Ghent University. https://lib.ugent.be/fulltxt/RUG01/002/273/594/RUG01-002273594_2016_0001_AC.pdf (last accessed September 2017). See as well: Johnstone, K. (2003). *Impro: improvisation and the theatre.* New York: Routledge. And: Spolin, V. (1999). *Improvisation for the theatre.* Evanston: Northwestern University Press.

114 Quinn, R.E. (2004). *Building the bridge as you walk on it: a guide for leading change.* Boston: Jossey-Bass.

Quotes

'We live in a constantly evolving environment in which it is impossible to know exactly what the future holds. We can best minimise and manage this risk by embracing uncertainty and being nimble enough to productively explore new ways of doing. Only agile organisations that embrace the new paradigm - which is defined by connectivity, big data and digitisation - will in future succeed. Future success will require the recognition of the abundance of new opportunities and resources, the co-creation of value with and for all stakeholders, and the empowering of employees with the clear responsibility and authority that motivates them to create innovative solutions that deliver exceptional results. This excellent must-read publication by Herman Van den Broeck and Barney Jordaan has admirably advanced our understanding of the crucial importance of the agility journey on which organisations need to embark.'

David Venter is professor at the University of Stellenbosch Business School and at the University of Cape Town Graduate School of Business, South Africa. He specialises in leadership and negotiation.

'The rapid pace of change that goes with digitalisation means that leaders and managers badly need to develop an agile attitude and approach to doing business. This book is one of the first I encountered that provides a coherent frame of reference that not only explains what agility is about, but which also provides techniques for implementing it in a sustainable way. While most management books 'prescribe' the same old recipes to meet modern day challenges, this book makes the reader question orthodox theories and approaches to leadership and management. It opens a new learning path for readers and their organisations. I really wish that every leader dares to accept the challenge of the authors to deeply reflect about the need for agility and how they can master that challenge. This will surely not only ensure to their survival but undoubtedly also ensure their growth!'

Steven Van Belleghem is a thought leader on the transformation of customer relationships and the future of marketing. He is an expert in inspiring companies to become true customer-centric organizations in this high speed digital world.

'Agility is key to sustainable performance of any company, whatever their size. Two third of Fortune 500 companies fall from the list in 20 years, mid-size companies are acquired because they do not move fast enough, and start-ups need always to balance agility and persistence. Herman Van den Broeck and Barney Jordaan's book is a must read for any leader, CEO and Board member. They offer provocative insights (none of them I disagree with!) which should stimulate questioning and profound change in many businesses.'

Roch Doliveux is chairman at GLG Institute and at the Board of Vlerick Business School. He is also honorary CEO at UCB.

'This is the type of book you should carry around with you: to browse, reflect and go back to frequently. It's the type of book to use as agile as the organisations it describes. You will find inspiration and wisdom on every single page.'

Marion Debruyne is dean of Vlerick Business School. Her interests lie at the intersection between marketing strategy, innovation and competition.

'*The Agile Leader's scrapbook* has a very original take on how leaders and organisations need to behave in today's hypercompetitive, ever changing business world. The book offers very useful tips on how leaders need to balance a learning orientation with an agile mindset to deal with challenges that constantly arise in the workplace. Being agile while trying to learn from challenges calls for leaders to not be wedded to established, anachronistic practices, but rather to be willing to take risks and embrace innovation.'

Deva Rangarajan is professor of marketing and associate director of the Center for Professional Selling at Miller College of Business, Indiana.

'Agility should be like the air we breathe for every entrepreneur. Smart start-ups 'attack' big companies for their lack of agility. By becoming bigger their first issue will be retaining their agility. Herman Van den Broeck and Barney Jordaans' book is an essential guide for every CEO of existing companies, but even more for every start-up to keep the right focus.'

Karel Van Eetvelt is CEO at Febelfin and at the Belgian Bankers' and Stockbroking Firms' Association.